CUSTOMER SUCCESS™

Beyond Customer Service To The Spirit of Enterprise Throughout the Ranks

B Y   B A R R Y   S .   F A R A H

BARON BOOKS

NEW YORK

FIRST EDITION

Designed by Mary Cukjati

printing number 2

Customer Success is a trademark of Barry S. Farah

Library of Congress Cataloging-in-Publication Data

Farah, Barry S.

Customer Success

p. cm.

ISBN 0-9665888-0-0

Baron Books titles may be purchased for business or promotional use or for special sales. For information, please write to:

Special Markets Department

Baron Books

590 Madison Avenue, 21st Floor

New York, N.Y. 10022

(212) 521-4470

Praise for Customer Success

WOW! I really do like this book. I will now always understand the difference between customer service and customer success. The clarity of thought demonstrated in this book to explain and convert a reader to drive to Customer Success is compelling. I thank you for giving me the opportunity to read it before my competitors. I plan to have our office heads read this book and teach it to our staff!

Brian D. Johnson, Vice Chairman & Chief Operating Officer Willis Corroon, KKR Associates. The World's Fourth Largest Risk Management and Insurance Consulting Firm

This is a bang-up, no-nonsense approach to business and Customer Success. The legion of business executives who desire the very best in dealing with their customers should read this book ASAP! Further, the sound advice provided by Barry Farah can make things fun again - whether in business or in life. This book is a winner!

H.E. Robertson, Brig. Gen., USAF (Ret), Consultant to heads of industry. Previously Public Affairs Director to the Chairman of Joint Chiefs of Staff and the Air Force Director of Public Affairs during Desert Shield/Desert Storm.

It was two steps beyond the theories of customer service that I have seen or heard about before hearing Barry Farah speak. I have used a lot of ideas since then. Many of VASA Brougher's clients have made very positive comments after hearing Barry Farah speak and requested several copies of the book. Personally I was impressed with Barry Farah's presentation and book. It is a very good combination. Mr. Farah is very convincing and consistent with the ideologies between the book and presentation. Mr Farah is very honest.

Roelof Konterman, President VASA Brougher, Inc. Major Industrial Insurance Organization

Customer Success is two parts practical business, one part genius. Barry's already-proven approach to customer retention is outlined here in an engaging, resourceful manner. This "winning mindset" is sure to produce a multitude of converts.

Ted Haggard, Senior Pastor
New Life Church (over 7,800 attendants)
National Association of Evangelicals and
Colorado Springs Association of Evangelicals Board Member

The book was an insightful and stimulating recipe for a dimension that industry has forgotten "The Customer". A quick, common sense fix that is an easy and entertaining read. A lesson in integrity and self-actualization.

Lawrence A. McLernon, Founder
Litel, InterActive MultiMedia NetWork and National Telecom

I made this book a mandatory reading assignment by all my employees. It was well received by our group and I have noticed the frequent use of the techniques by my employees. Barry Farah has put the information in a way that is easily understood and thereby used.

Bill Lindsey, President
GreenTree Administrators, Inc.

Best book on Customer Service I have ever read. To compare Farah's theories and practice to the "customer service" I typically receive seems unfair to Mr. Farah and this landmark work. I am glad that Farah renamed the concept and hope that this term will catch on. This primer on serving customers with a constant eye toward helping them succeed is critical to anyone operating a business! I have tried many of Farah's strategies, and found that they work!

Paul T. Moore, President and Chief Executive Officer
Millennium Market

Acknowledgments

I am grateful to my wife, Tamra, for her encouragement, advice and organizational assistance. She's not only gorgeous, but smart. I want to thank Randy Welsch and Paul Moore for dropping everything to read and edit the book. Their assistance was essential.

My staff produces excellent work. They have kept the business humming while I was engaged in this effort. Special mention goes to Jeff Leffew and Bob Devens for outstanding collaboration in protecting me from unnecessary distractions while I wrote this book. David Kennedy rendered useful strategic counsel, while David Hoeft preached my own sermon to me, challenging me to get it done now, rather than later.

A heart felt thanks to my entire staff for their dedication and loyalty. What a great customer success team!

To my Employees.

*They make customer success
a reality in our business.*

Table of Contents

❧

Preface

❧

C ustomer success is really a mindset. Mine developed from years of observation.

It seems like I have always had customers. In elementary school years, I sold everything from Christmas cards to flashlights door-to-door. In junior high, I squeezed my own lawn care business in between soccer games. In high school, I owned a profitable landscaping business, sold siding, vacuum cleaners, water treatment equipment and steel buildings. I had all the sales kits in my car - just kind of depended on what you needed and I'd whip out the right one. During my college years I owned a tree-trimming, landscaping and remodeling business.

By the time I obtained my undergraduate degree at 21, it seemed I had experienced a full business career, but there was much more to learn. My experience at IBM trained me in people management and my MBA education disciplined my thinking. My tenure at Ford Motor Company taught me financial analysis, while my management consulting experience strengthened strategic planning and problem solving skills. I felt equipped to settle in and run a business for the long haul. In 1991, I launched The Personnel Department, Inc.

I wanted to establish more than just a business. I wanted an overriding vision to guide my lofty growth objectives. Don't get me wrong. I was very profit-motivated. I simply wanted to create a corporate culture that would truly help my customers in exceptional ways.

I also wanted to create an environment where everyone could grow, where employees did not feel like *employees*. I don't believe in an egalitarian environment, but I wanted my people to have an opportunity to exceed even their own dreams. I wanted a company that was bursting with energy and highly respected.

The results so far have met my expectations. Through 1996 our company enjoyed 100% customer retention. Since then, growth has continued to explode. For example, first quarter revenues for 1998 were 65% higher than first quarter revenues for 1997. We have clients in 27 states and three countries. During our rapid growth phase we experienced some growing pains, but we continue to enjoy a near perfect customer retention record.

Though we have succeeded on paper, the achievement I am most proud of is watching a spirit of enterprise flourish in our people. When I visit customers, they often comment on the integrity, professionalism and sincere service-orientation of our team.

That is not to say we have done everything perfect. Some business principles were learned by scraping my nose on the concrete. For example, the admonitions found in Focused Alliances (see Part One, *Principle Based Business*) come from what I learned about my penchant to explore new markets. I attempted to expand into the temporary services business and got skinned.

The concepts presented in this book have been thoroughly tested by experience in the marketplace. The Personnel Department is a Professional Employer Organization (PEO). A PEO may be one of the more difficult service businesses to operate. Though each PEO is different, we are a culmination of seven service businesses: government compliance, human resources, payroll administration, benefits administration, risk management, legal counsel and business consulting. To render our services, precision is demanded.

This book is divided into three parts, Establishing a Foundation for Customer Success, Toward a Customer Success Mindset and Customer Success is Self Sustaining. In Part One, we define customer success, provoke you to consider the principles and present a superior corporate strategy for your organization.

The foundation prepares you for Part Two, which discusses the need for training. We provide specific tips for hiring the right people. Then we discuss how to develop the culture and mindset of customer success within your company.

Finally, Part Three presents an avenue for making customer success self sustaining. First, we analyze the concept of 100% customer retention. Then, we discuss a customer success guarantee. Finally, we provide our view of how cohesion at the top protects and defends the customer success environment.

I am not a consultant handing out esoteric concepts. This book represents what we have actually done.

As you read through these ideas, you might think they are impossible to implement in your enterprise. If you give them a chance, however, I think you will find room for this approach in your organization. My goal is not to placate you by rehashing what you already know, but to challenge and provoke you to greater degrees of success. I hope this book propels you beyond customer service toward a winning mindset!

Introduction

ﻬ

Customer service is the mantra in modern business culture. In my view, customer service is an inferior business focus, yielding mediocre results at best. **Customer success** will render less customer service and the customer will be more satisfied.

Customer service is reactionary by nature and is usually treated by business leaders as a necessary evil — the cost of 'doing business'. If customers appear content with your service, or aren't complaining about it, most managers are thrilled.

Customer success, on the other hand, establishes a higher standard. When properly ingrained in your employees, it sends a powerful message to customers that motivates them to come back to you for more. As the mindset is injected into your corporate culture, it is like an avalanche careening down a mountain. It builds its own momentum, creating excitement in your customers and your employees.

ﻬ

Customer success...is like an avalanche careening down a mountain. It builds its own momentum, creating excitement in your customers and your employees.

Customer service often tends to be superficial, insincere and reactionary. **Customer success** argues for a proactive, more meaningful alternative. It provides the tools necessary to equip an employee mindset which motivates innovative and diligent problem solving on behalf of the customer.

In today's culture there is a limit to how far we will go in serving others. Most of us are preoccupied with serving ourselves. This can be reflected in the customer service environment. There isn't a driving motivation to "do a back flip" to serve the customer, but rather a push to get the customer "off your plate". We need something to catapult us past our natural tendency toward lethargy.

This book does not attempt to fix our cultural situation. It simply acknowledges it and presents a better vision for the employee, empowering him to stand out from the crowd.

Customer success does not require profound intelligence or even a lot of extra time. It does demand active leadership. I can say from experience that it results in a powerful, energizing and fun corporate culture that can captivate the loyalty of your customers.

This book will help you approach your customers with new vigor. It ultimately argues on behalf of releasing the creative inventor inside of each employee. Every payroll processor, benefits administrator, auto mechanic, carpenter, marketing manager, accountant, and executive possesses an untapped creative component inside of them that wants to really make an impact in helping people to solve their problems. Our job is to fan the flames of this powerful drive and unleash it.

PART ONE

CUSTOMER SUCCESS

Establishing a Foundation
for Customer Success

Have you noticed the increase in customer service books? Ever wondered why we don't have an increase in customer service?

One reason is because customer service is hard work — too hard for most managers to sustain. Customer service actually requires more work than **customer success**. The success of a customer service program is almost entirely dependent on the management team's ability to convey and enforce the rules. *Customer success requires leadership, but it manages itself.*

In some situations, the outward behavior of a **customer success** representative would vary only slightly from that of a customer service representative. However, what is transpiring inside the employee's mind is radically different.

Customer Success — Beyond Customer Service

Customer success is enterprising, bold and dynamic. It fosters ingenuity and inventiveness. The **customer success** employee is personally in control of his work. As a result, the **customer success** representative is more than an employee. He is an *associate*, a professional in a firm, a partner-in-training. He is filled with purpose. By definition, he is bounding with initiative and energy. **Customer success** representatives are more ambitious, more resourceful and having more fun than the typical customer service employee.

Here's why. The **customer success** discipline helps foster an environment that celebrates the truly innovative. These employees are not waiting for a flash of brilliance. They are simply *determined to* create and develop new services or products that meet their customer's needs.

> These employees are not waiting for a flash of brilliance. They are simply determined to create and develop new services or products that meet their customer's needs.

In this chapter we will discuss the meaning of **customer success**. **Seven components** define the passion to help a customer succeed. I use the term **customer success** as an active verb. It does not wait for problems. It fixes them before they arise.

1. Discover Your Customer's Values & History

Customer success invests more time during the initial stages of a customer relationship. We view this as customer orientation. One of the first questions we ask a new customer is why they purchased our service. We ask why they bought from us instead of the competition. This provides insight into how we can serve the customer according to the customer's priorities.

> I use the term customer success as an active verb. It does not wait for problems. It fixes them before they arise.

Customer service simply responds to its knowledge of the present situation. If selling to businesses, **customer success** wants to learn about the company's values, the technology they employ, how long they have been in business, and so forth. It will understand the ownership structure, the corporate philosophy, mission, vision and values. It will discover how many people the business employs and what its plans are for the future. It will find the level to which the company has accomplished its goals in the past, particularly as it relates to the service or product provided. It will also explore the expectations for this business relationship.

Customer success will ask, "What would we need to do to cause the use of our services to be one of the best business decisions you have made? How would that differ from the last vendor's performance?"

In retail, **customer success** will seek to understand the customer's demographics and preferences. An example can be found in the travel industry. Any travel agent can put together a vacation package. A **customer success** agent will tailor make it to suit the need.

Customer service would be satisfied with a general profile: the customer prefers four star accommodations, a non-smoking room with a king-size bed and a roll away for the munchkin. **Customer success** would ask more questions. "What was your favorite vacation? Describe the food, entertainment and accommodations. What kind of memories would you like to build while you are on your next vacation? Are you interested in a more restful or lively experience?"

Customer success is interested in the values of the person being served. Your customer may define fast-paced night-life as enjoyable or he may be socially conservative, with a traditional family and young children. In this case, he probably would not prefer a vacation on the beach in Francais de Bois — even if you can offer him an inexpensive vacation package there. As an agent, you need to know that this city has focused on recruiting nude sunbathers. It would be difficult for a family to spend a few days on the beach there without being shocked by such indiscretion. A vacation that would be acceptable to someone else, could be a disaster for your customer and his family.

It will have asked enough open-ended questions to be equipped to proactively make the customer's experience exceptional.

If this story makes you want to judge someone, hold your fire. I am talking about the importance of knowing the customer's values, not imposing yours. I purposely selected an example that could generate debate. Knowing the customer's history and values requires you to suppress your own.

Customer success will have a general grasp of the major disappointments the customer has experienced in the past. It will have asked enough open-ended questions to be equipped to proactively make the customer's experience exceptional. It focuses on his definition, his values, his preferences. It does not try to fashion the customer into its description of what is fun, pleasant or smart business. It helps the customer uncover his. Knowing the customer's values and history is really knowing his story.

2. Anticipate Your Customer's *Real* Needs

C ustomer service handles questions and issues when the customer calls. That's nice, but I think it is much better to anticipate the problem before he calls. **Customer success** anticipates the customer's need before it arises. Realistically, how can this be done? Here's an example.

Our services are provided primarily to companies with less than 200 employees. (For a fuller explanation, please see the Preface). Most of these businesses are privately held and run by an entrepreneur. One of the services we provide is payroll administration. The most common pay date is Friday.

When Thanksgiving rolls around, most entrepreneurs are not thinking about payroll logistics. Even the person responsible for providing us with the payroll inputs is too busy to consider that the inputs must be provided early if the employees are to receive their checks on Wednesday.

We call the week before and say, "I know you usually provide us with payroll inputs on Monday, but if I could get those from you earlier you won't have to worry about it next week and I'll have the paychecks ready for you before you take off for Thanksgiving." The customer says, "Oh, my gosh, is it already Thanksgiving? I thought we were still in October. Great idea. I'm glad you called."

Taking this extra two minutes with them in advance can save them and us hours of time trying to fix a problem later. The alternative would be to provide a lot of customer service during the week of Thanksgiving. When we think about what the customer *might need* based on what we know, we can actually reduce the amount of reactive service we have to provide.

A customer service environment reacts only to the customer's verbalized needs. **Customer success** goes beyond this and proactively assesses what the customer *really* needs to succeed.

The customer success representative allocates energy and thought toward identifying the genuine needs of the customer before the customer calls.

This includes delving into the things that the customer may not be aware he needs. Even if the customer initiates the inquiry or registers a complaint, the **customer success** representative will be better equipped to turn the call into a productive and meaningful discussion. She has a better chance of having thought through the customer's inquiry before he called. Through experience and forethought she understands what the customer will need and is ready for most of the challenges that she will encounter.

The **customer success** representative allocates energy and thought toward identifying the genuine needs of the customer before the customer calls. When the customer calls, the representative is able to confidently and swiftly address the need of the moment and solve the problem of the hour.

---

3. Address Customer's Symptoms — Focus on the Cause

Customer service is primarily defensive. The customer calls with a problem and the representative is on the run. He may handle the issue at hand with composure, but then he just sits there waiting for the next question. The **customer success** representative avoids "reaction mode". She answers the question, but quickly turns her attention toward deeper issues.

> *Where customer service may put a band-aide on the wound, customer success will first clean it out.*

Customer success looks for the right opportunity to go to the next level. It is thinking, "What caused this problem in the first place?" **Customer success** is looking for the real culprit, while still solving the problem on the surface that the customer presented. The representative is really the project leader, properly provoking the customer to help drive the process and to uncover the best and most correct solution. The customer becomes a participant in a productive problem-solving endeavor.

Where customer service may put a band-aide on the wound, **customer success** will first clean it out. In the **customer success** environment, the representative is mostly on offense. It starts out with a defensive play, responding to the customer's inquiry, but it quickly moves to a productive attack on the source of the problem.

I realize this flies in the face of methodology at some help desks. The major performance criteria for many customer service representatives is how quickly they can get a customer off the phone. I understand that time is money, but we are talking about the customer's time, not ours. In the long term, the customer spends less time with

CUSTOMER SUCCESS — BEYOND CUSTOMER SERVICE

a **customer success** representative. A customer service representative may get the customer off the phone quickly, but if they do not have the best solution, the customer will simply need to call again.

Customer service focuses on *answering* questions, but may miss the point. **Customer success** focuses on *asking* questions. It is bent on uncovering the source of the distress.

---

4. Do a Back Flip

There really is not that much in business that is impossible. We just need a **customer success** bias.

For example, one of our **customer success** representatives was hit with a service emergency late on a Friday afternoon. She was the only employee in the office. The customer, in a distant city, had not received their payroll checks. The customer's employees were irate. The overnight shipper had failed. The checks were somewhere between Indianapolis and Atlanta.

Our **customer success** representative did a back flip. She wired money directly into each of the seventeen employees' bank accounts. For those without bank accounts, she had cash delivered to their home. She never mentioned that it was not our "fault." She followed up with cards to each of the customer's employees and flowers and a box of chocolates to the customer.

> I understand that time is money, but we are talking about the customer's time, not ours.

An adequate solution would have been to allow the customer to receive their paychecks on the next business day. After all, it was quittin' time. Mediocre solutions are often satisfactory to the customer service representative.

The "back flip" mentality does not require an emergency to show off. It *probes* for an even better solution to the customer's problem. Though this requires more effort, overall, it really doesn't take a lot more time. It utilizes the problem solving schematic detailed in Part Two, *Customer Success Training*.

Often customer service representatives get so caught up in the quagmire of the problem that *relief* is the only positive emotion they feel when they get the customer off of the phone. Short term, that may make sense, but it is not **customer success**. The better discovery may require only a few more minutes of discussion and effort, but results in a more potent solution.

5. Lead Your Customer

Make yourself an expert on what your customer needs before he knows he needs it. Then lead him down the best path. Reorganize your service offering in ways that are relevant to the success of your customer. Develop a list of questions that help the customer discover what he really wants. You, not the customer, are the expert in your field.

She is leading with knowledge-based questions.

Consider a waitress in a three star restaurant. "What'll ya have?" is customer service. A **customer success** waitress would have asked tactful questions about what kind of dining *experience* you would prefer. She would be well-versed on the menu and proper combinations. When the customer asks, "What's good here?"

She would not say, "Everything, hon', kinda depends on what ya want." That puts it back in the customer's lap. **Customer success** never puts responsibility back into the hands of the customer prematurely.

Customer success is much more helpful. The waitress says, "Tonight we are offering three different types of dining experiences though our menu reflects fifteen entree choices. Are you in the mood for a spicy and hot plate, a full-bodied dish or a rich and creamy taste for your main entree?" The leading questions help the customer determine what he wants through the process of elimination. If the customer chooses spicy, then the waitress could *lead* the customer through the five entrees that are spicy. She would not say, "We have fish, pork and chicken. What'll it be?"

Reorganize your service offering in ways that are relevant to the success of your customer.

She is leading with knowledge-based questions, helping you decide precisely what kind of dining experience you want. You have made the decisions with the expert guidance of the **customer success** representative. And you thought she was just a waitress!

You might be thinking, "You can't be serious. Do you know how long this would take to train a waitress in this manner, not to mention the time it takes to delve into the specific interest of the customers at each table?"

First, training your people on product knowledge is critical to enlarging their job. The waitress is not just a server. She is in charge of engineering successful dining experiences. She now feels smart and competent. The result: you have reduced your employee turnover. The reduction in recruiting, and retraining costs will more than cover the cost of the training.

Second, her thoughtful guiding of the customer may take a bit more time on the front end, but not much. Look around the next time you go to a restaurant. The waitress can spend a lot of time at each table trying to get the order because she is *answering questions.* Why is she answering questions? So the customer can figure out what he wants! It does not take much more time for the waitress to be asking the questions. During the meal, the chance of a customer sending back a reject because "it was not what they expected" is dramatically reduced. By allocating more energy on the front end, the waitress will spend less time over the course of the meal.

The issue is simple. Customers know their preferences. But they are not experts in the product or service being rendered. They need to be thoughtfully led. Customer service answers questions. **Customer success** takes the lead. It thoughtfully asks questions to lead the customer down the path to an exceptional service experience.

6. Be Quick & Agile

Speed is an important element of the **customer success** environment. Our goal is to provide extremely quick response time to each customer inquiry. This starts with answering the phone in person. I understand the financial arguments for having automated voice response, but it often takes customers too long to get through the phone maze in order to get a problem resolved. Speed does not mean rushing the customer. It means rushing to serve the customer. It means returning the call when you promised — or sooner — always opting for now, rather than later, to address a problem.

You can no longer manage a business solely on maintaining cash or gaining market-share. To thrive we must manage our business to optimize time. Speed honors this reality, providing accurate and appropriate help, fast.

Agility produces solutions that anticipate and overcome customer obstacles. You do not want the service desk to inform you that you must call another department. "Wait a minute!", you say to yourself. "I thought I called customer service. Why aren't they handling this for me?" Do you want to know why? The representative does not want to be put on hold while waiting for that other department to answer, either.

> Speed does not mean rushing the customer. It means rushing to serve the customer.

Agility fixes corporate bottlenecks, forcing employees to face internal frustrations on behalf of the customer. **Customer success** will never be satisfied with giving a customer a phone number to another department and getting that customer off her plate. The **customer success** representative will call the other office for the customer, find the right person to talk to and patch the customer through. Or it will solve the problem for the customer and then she will call the customer back and report the results.

An obstacle is something that gets in the way of your customer achieving a goal. A **customer success** representative is like a great hurdles runner who will glide over obstacles with athletic splendor. A **customer success** environment requires maneuvering around difficulties on behalf of the customer. The agile representative would never frustrate the customer by making him wind through the maze of her corporate bureaucracy.

7. Be Humble & Diligent

Customer success is also *humble*. Taking a humble position has never been popular. **Customer success** is more interested in fixing the problem than placing blame. The **customer success** representative will take a personal hit and even lose face to make the customer better off.

> The customer success representative will take a personal hit and even lose face to make the customer better off.

A good customer service program could be fast, agile and humble, but rarely is it *diligent*. **Customer success** is grounded in perseverance. It will not give up until it gets to the bottom of the real problem and renders the best solution. Customer service is usually satisfied when the customer is content — or at least off the phone!

This concept is illustrated by recreational hikers and mountain climbers. In Colorado we have over fifty mountains that exceed 14,000 feet. Many of them have trails than can be hiked by an amateur. Often a novice climber will quit before reaching the summit of one of these majestic peaks.

What is startling to me is that most quit at around 13,500 feet. They get tired of being faked-out by the "false peaks", and the view seems good enough at 13,500 anyway. (False peaks are those places that look like the top peak as you are climbing them, but they are really just a rise in elevation that blocks your view of the real peak.) With a little more effort, one last push, they could reach the top and enjoy a 360 degree, 200 mile view.

I find service representatives to be similar. They weaken quickly.

They are satisfied with an adequate solution. They do not persevere.

A **customer success** environment is not measured by how many customers are content and therefore not bothering you. Rather, it is assessed by the degree to which a customer's business or life is running better.

The Cost of Customer Success

You might be thinking that the **customer success** environment is too much work. Is it really worth it to shift from a customer service to a **customer success** mindset?

Remember the last time you were treated poorly at a department store? Recently, a customer service representative leaned across the counter, and looked at me with a lazy glare that almost dared me to go to a competitor. He didn't want to engage in the *exercise of thinking* to solve my problem. After a limited effort he said, "That's all I can do."

I tried to reason with him, even attempted to do the thinking for him. I wanted to leave the store and try out a competitor, but it was too inconvenient.

So, I did a back flip to get him to help me. My efforts with this customer service representative were in vain. The lights were on, but no one was home.

So, *I* did a back flip to get *him* to help me. My efforts with this customer service representative were in vain. The lights were on, but no one was home.

As I contemplated his behavior, I was struck by how easy it would have been to keep me as a customer. If he had just possessed the right mindset. Certainly he had been thoroughly trained in his company's nationally respected customer service program. I saw it on his face, and felt it in the air: he did not just forget the duties of customer service — he never had the *vision* for **customer success**.

That day a famous department store lost a good customer and they will probably never know why. Customer service did not cut the mustard.

Have you ever calculated the real cost of replacing a good customer? There is the marketing replacement cost, the operational disruption and the enormous toll on corporate goodwill. The rule of thumb used to be that an unsatisfied customer might tell 10 to 12 people about his bad experience. Now, with the internet, they can share the bad news with literally thousands of people.

Recently, I received an email from someone I do not know. This individual conveyed how she had been treated poorly by a well known store. To retaliate she included one of this establishment's famed cookie recipes that it sells for $250. She strongly urged everyone on the receiving end of her email to forward this message to as many people as possible. Who knows how many of them forwarded the cookie recipe on to their friends and family. And those folks could send it to others, and on it goes. There could easily be thousands of people that know of this recipe and her ill-will toward this store.

On the other hand, if a customer is thrilled with your services they may tell two to five people. Why the disparity? Anger is a strong emotion and it moves people to action. Happiness just stimulates someone to sit back and enjoy his experience.

There Is a Difference

In summary, **customer success** delves into the mind of the customer. It goes beyond empathy. Empathy understands the customer from the customer's point of view. That's a good start, but not enough. **Customer success** analyzes what will catapult the customer to the next level.

Customer success is extraordinarily proactive. It anticipates what the customer will need, in many cases prior to the customer's knowledge of their own need.

Customer success also engages the emotions and yields a positive experience for everyone involved. It is not limited to the well-worn sermons on customer service. To provide the customer with outstanding service of the wrong thing does not make him successful. The corporate ambition should be simple: anticipate the customer's real needs and provide genuine solutions which assist the customer beyond his expectations.

> To provide the customer with outstanding service of the wrong thing does not make him successful.

A customer service organization is tempted to let whatever is happening today dictate results. The **customer success** endeavor is attentive to the opportunities available and it seizes the day. As a result, the **customer success** representative can deliver service that causes others to marvel. In reality she is simply going about her duties with the customer's success in mind.

The culmination of the **customer success** environment can be seen in the following example from the retail world.

An Example from the Retail World

How does one implement the **customer success** strategy in a retail environment? Well, let's pick perhaps one of the most competitive retail industries in existence — the auto repair shop. This is a tough business. When a customer comes to you, it is because she is mad. Something isn't working right.

In addition, the industry has been tarnished by scam artists. Since customers have heard of those horror stories, they come to you with suspicion in their eyes. To compound your problem, there are ga-zillions of honest competitors. So, it is not as simple as waving a banner and saying, "We're the good guys, honest."

A **customer success** driven company directs the overall strategy. You cannot effectively implement **customer success** half way. Here are some ideas of how I would run an auto repair shop.

First, I would have an extremely clean facility. The cleanest part of the facility would be the inviting waiting area. There would be a nice place for the kids to play and read books in a separate room with rubber-padded walls and floor. This would include educational videos for math, science and English. That room would have sound-proof glass, but an intercom system allows an adult to plug in the headphones in the adult area and listen in at any time. Want to listen to your kids? Simply plug in the headphones and turn to Channel One.

Would you prefer not to listen to your kids? You would rather listen to classical music and read *Democracy in America*? Fine, get the book off the shelf and turn to Channel Two. You have ten choices. Enjoy your time.

The layout would be the opposite of what you have often encountered, where you had to wade through a pile of tires to get to the customer service counter. When you walk in you are greeted with the circular **customer success** and information booth. After you explain your car problem the well-groomed and knowledgeable employee says, "We will handle everything, Ms. Jones. Allow me to escort you to the children's play area." This employee takes an additional four minutes with the customer. Four minutes!!! And she wins the customer for life.

She explains the coffee and cinnamon roll honor system, the variety of reading materials available, the intercom system for the kids' room, and in which lane to look for her car. Finally, she puts the customer totally at ease, "I hope you enjoy your stay, but we will endeavor to get you on your way as soon as possible. A *transportation repair specialist* will come to you in a few minutes with a diagnosis of your automobile's problems. We will then describe how long it will take for us to fix the problem. If we are off on our estimate by more than thirty minutes — the excess is on us! In the mean time, if you have any questions, please do not hesitate to ask."

You smell fresh brewed coffee, hot apple cider and freshly baked cinnamon rolls. I would charge for this and let the customer pay on an honor system. I want you to smell cinnamon, not grease.

The adult area is exceptionally comfortable and strategically located between the kids' area and the workshop. This adult area has access to a small library of current trade journals and great works of literature, including the Federalist Papers, Shakespeare and Alexis de Toqueville. Or you can hook up your laptop to one of the several power sources and access your email or finish up a report. The library, trade journal subscriptions and telephone lines might only cost a few thousand dollars, but I would more than make that up in lower marketing costs and slightly higher prices. I want the customer to enjoy an experience — they should be almost disappointed when the car is fixed so soon!

If you absolutely cannot wait in my "club" atmosphere waiting room, you can use one of my four or five courtesy cars. I would charge you enough to cover wear and tear and fuel — no base line cost, just a per mile expense. If you have to get somewhere and all the cars are out — I'll take you myself. Remember, I have to model exceptional **customer success**.

I would hire the best mechanics in town. They would know how to diagnose problems accurately, and they would be the best at fixing them. The mechanics would be in nice looking uniforms. The design would be sharp and classy, not corny. I am trying to impress both the customer and the mechanic. We have exceptionally high standards. Tighten that nut one extra time, be conscientious. Perfection is expected.

The company logo would be on the front of the shirt and some snappy **customer success** motto would be neatly placed on the back. I want each customer and employee to see that motto. All my employees would have their hair nicely trimmed, and would be required to come to work clean-shaven. They would all go through a one-day charm school. "Yes ma'am, yes sir, please, and thank you" would be required work rules. (Yes, that is legal.)

It does not matter if there is a shortage of mechanics. Pay is important and these would be among the highest paid mechanics in town. But what is really attracting them and keeping them is their pride in participating in our corporate success. They are part of the "elite."

Quickly, the word will get out — the best benefit package and incentive system and work environment is at my shop. If you are an exceptional mechanic, and if you qualify, you might be considered.

I would have sound-proof glass separating the waiting room from the work shop area. The waiting room is quiet, but it does offer visibility. The workshop would be at a 30-degree angle from the waiting room, so a customer could easily see his car, if desired. The employees would know they are always being watched, but not heard by the customer. I would train the employees on how to work hard and make it fun. They would not be permitted to swear, but they would be encouraged to shout clean jokes. The customer who is looking in sees a lot of fast working, energetic, clean-cut mechanics with big smiles.

The result: you have enjoyed an experience and will come back for more. As the shop owner, I didn't just fix your car — your kids are better educated. You enjoyed an excellent cinnamon roll and read something that made you a richer person! Or you completed a project on your laptop.

As we graciously explain your invoice, we describe in detail all the duties we performed. The work is guaranteed. We did not just adjust your brakes. We have secured that your transportation will be safe. You *reluctantly* leave my shop to get into your car — it's spotless! The radio is not blaring on some rap station. To the contrary, you find a little mint on the dash attached to a handwritten note. "Thanks for coming in! We wish you safe and pleasant travels."

Yes, I would charge slightly more than anyone else on the street. Do you think you'd come back? Will you tell your friends?

Principle Based Business

Ask the average person on the street what they think is the purpose of business. The answers can be summed up in one word: Profit. To enjoy a profit a business must be managed in a sensible fashion. You certainly must have realistic plans in place. You can't sell the product below cost or provide a service that no one wants to purchase. Your business must be based on pragmatism with a clear eye toward the bottom line. Right?

> One of the most pragmatic decisions a business leader can make is to build his business on a set of unchangeable principles.

I disagree. Pragmatism is essential, but subservient to principle. The business based on a pragmatic approach alone possesses a glaring vulnerability. Although a pragmatic approach is exceptional at exploiting profit opportunities, it may violate important principles which will undermine its ultimate success. One of the most pragmatic decisions a business leader can make is to build his business on a set of unchangeable principles. This decision will produce several rewards.

A business based on principles is safe. It provides a sound environment for my associates. They won't be asked to lie or cook the books. They won't be reprimanded for turning away business in the process of practicing appropriate ethics. They know why we do what we do.

A business based on principle provides more satisfying job content for its employees. We can't possibly train an employee how to handle every type of problem or issue they will encounter. We *can* train them to act on principle. As long as an associate makes decisions from that foundation, she has a better chance of rendering a successful solution for the customer. An associate can navigate uncharted waters with confidence. We will support her decision because we will always champion our principles.

A business based on principle makes it through economic downturns. When the economy is booming everyone succeeds to some extent. When times are tough, customers prefer to deal with reliable, tested businesses. Customers desire to purchase from an enterprise that modifies its business strategy to accommodate the customer's needs, not one that alters business principles to satisfy its own greed.

A business based on principle can manage projects which have never been attempted. Most successful business relationships require innovation after the sale. During the "request for proposal" stage the real question the customer needs to have answered is, "What will the project leader's decision-making process be when encountering the unknown?" A principled approach provides the basis for an enduring trust between you and your customer when unforeseen challenges arise.

Seven Principles for Business Success

The diagram below reflects seven Business Principles on which my business is built. The principles are Customer Success Philosophy, Business Philosophy, Mission, Vision & Values, Destroy Politics, Communications, Focused Alliances and Authority & Risk. When all of the components are properly functioning together, our business will be successful, culminating in the capstone of the Spirit of Enterprise Throughout the Ranks.

Though success to us is larger than generating a profit through a pragmatic approach, we do wish to win in the marketplace. We aggressively pursue opportunities for financial gain.

1. Customer Success Philosophy

"Get out and really listen to your customers."
— *Robert W. Galvin, 1988*

The foundation is the starting place in the construction of a building. If the foundation is perfectly level and plumb, then the rest of the building can be rock solid. From a well-placed foundation, a Sistine Chapel or Empire State Building can be constructed.

The foundation principle of a business seems intangible, but its impact on the success of an enterprise is real. It is an authentic philosophy that employees can sink their teeth into. Everyone in the company knows the business is based on this foundation.

The first step in establishing our business foundation is the **customer success** philosophy. When we build upon this concept, everything else fits into place. This first principle is a mindset that permeates everything we do. It is how we render a hospitable environment to our only real corporate asset — the customer.

This principle transcends the difficulties of everyday business. The **customer success** philosophy is critical to our way of thinking and our whole approach to every business decision. It is our bedrock principle. Our **customer success** philosophy was fully elaborated in Part One, *Customer Success — Beyond Customer Service.* The summary paragraph we use to explain this to our employees and customers follows:

Customer Success
Philosophy Summary

Our Company philosophy includes a primary focus on the success of the customer. This concept extends beyond the well-worn sermons on customer service. To provide the customer with outstanding service of the wrong thing does not make him/her successful. Our ambition is to anticipate the customer's real needs and provide genuine solutions which assist the customer beyond his/her expectations. Customer success is not a formula—it is a mindset.

2. Business Philosophy

"For whoever aids the society of men by his industry…is not to be reckoned among the idle." — *John Calvin, 1548*

Upon the perfectly sound foundation of **customer success**, our Business Philosophy is established. Our business philosophy includes a desire to pursue a profit and win in the marketplace. But it is much more. As we discuss in Part Two, we communicate it to our employees, prospects and customers, enabling them to understand what to expect from the way we do business.

This philosophy contributes to our success in two ways. First, it provides accountability to our business leaders. For example, we say that we believe in a conservative debt load. Any customer can come to our office and look at our audited financial statements and see that we practice what we preach. Because of our business philosophy, my CFO is compelled to ensure that our debt loads are conservative - and he does a great job, by the way.

Second, it keeps our employees consistent. They have confidence to make intelligent business decisions. They do not have to apologize for any business conduct as long as it conforms to our business philosophy. Here's ours:

Business Philosophy

We believe in fundamental business ethics. In essence, we believe in treating vendors, trusted advisors, customers and employees in the same way we would want them to treat us.

We believe in the spirit of enterprise. We should enjoy delivering exceptional business solutions and relish winning in the marketplace.

We believe in persistence. Every business problem we have encountered has had a solution. The faint-hearted quit moments before the sale is closed or the innovation is discovered.

We believe in planning and analyzing the potential consequences of all business decisions, but we reject indecision due to lack of information. We believe that business acumen factors the intuitive into the decision process. The left brain is important, but it is only half of the brain.

We believe in conservative debt loads. We reject the high leverage approach to operating a business, since it carries unnecessary risks to both our employees and customers.

We believe in simplicity and common sense. We believe in focusing on the core services of our business, not being distracted by the vast array of diversification possibilities. We like to ask the questions: What can we deliver better than anyone else? What do our customers say about how well we are serving them?

We believe in leadership. We will seek intelligent counsel, but ultimately decisions have to be made. The one who makes the decision should have total authority and responsibility for the consequences of the decision. We believe leadership is being the head servant to our customers and employees.

We believe in serving our Customers with 100% accuracy. We believe quality is achievable the first time. We believe the intelligent use of automation is helpful, but the key to accuracy is genuine concern for the Customer's well-being.

We believe it is our fault if our Staff is not equipped with the tools to have a passion for serving the Customer with excellence. It is our responsibility to train them thoroughly and provide them with incentive and reward systems which will motivate them to embrace this attitude.

We believe that most everyone works below their potential. As a result, we will provide increasing levels of responsibility to our Staff. This approach obviously benefits everyone.

We believe in the effective stewardship of time and money. Effectiveness is often doing first things first, and second things not at all. In other words, resist the allure of easy lower priority tasks.

3. Mission, Vision & Values

"Without a vision, the people perish." — *Proverbs 29:18*

The final foundational principle is contained in our Mission, Vision and Values. The sales related objectives in a vision statement will change over time. However, the type of company we envision is as lasting and timeless as granite.

In my view, values are perhaps the most important component of this business principle. We are so keen on maintaining our values that our sales staff has permission to make the following statement during a sales presentation: "As you can see, this represents our mission, vision and values. Here's the CEO's direct telephone number. This will get you past the receptionist, straight to his office. If you ever sense that one of our employees has strayed from these values, or if we do not succeed in properly demonstrating these values, please contact the CEO immediately. He will want to talk to you. It is that important to us."

> ...the customer comes first. The customer always trumps our personal schedule.

In essence, our values highlight the Golden Rule: "Treat others as you want them to treat you." In practical terms, if we are making a decision in the middle of the day between serving the customer or getting something done on our "to do" list, the customer comes first. The customer always trumps our personal schedule.

The need for a company mission statement is clear. It defines the overall reason why you are conducting business. It provides an avenue for all of your customers and all of your people to know why you do what you do.

We strive to set our customers free to focus on *their* vision. Some of our customers have quadrupled the value of their business since using our services. It is hard to believe, but some of them have told us that we deserve much of the credit for their outstanding accomplishments.

The mission, vision and values provide the employees with more than just a job and a paycheck. It instills in them an excitement about their role in our organization.

Mission

We will be the premier provider of professional employer services! We will continually elevate the level of products and services our customers enjoy. These firms will experience increased success as a result of our world class personnel administration services, human resource assistance and business counsel. Our mission is to set the customer free to succeed, unencumbered by the duties we fulfill.

Vision

We will become a great company by the year 2000. In the personnel administration industry our name will be synonymous with excellence. In the markets we serve we will be thought of as a standard for professional employment. When business people talk about professional employer services they will interchange our name, The Personnel Department, with their descriptions. As XEROX is used to explain copying or KLEENEX is used to describe tissue, The Personnel Department and its affiliates will be used to describe the concept of outsourcing personnel functions and structuring employer related strategic alliances.

Some of the most well known businesses in the world will be using our services. Some of the top performers in the INC 500 will mention that using our services enabled them to accomplish their explosive growth.

We will receive unsolicited phone calls and letters from customers, customer employees and trusted advisors who say, "Thank you for being in business: your serviceability is exceptional and your integrity is valued." Our employees will claim this is the best place they have ever worked. Trade journal writers will claim our company serves customers the best. At the end of the year 2000, our combined companies will have over $100 million in gross revenues.

Values

- Customer satisfaction requires an entrepreneurial back flip.

- Integrity is not to be compromised: be honest, fair, consistent.

- Commitments made must be fulfilled.

- Never cut corners, get the details right, the first time. Care about the solution.

- Be humble — don't dominate, don't judge, don't gossip.

- Do unto others as you would have them do unto you.

- I own the mistake, but we fix it together.

- We share the glory, but I excel individually.

4. Destroy Politics

"Politics are usually the executive expression of human immaturity."
— *Vera Brittain, 1933*

With our solid foundation of Customer Success, Business Philosophy and Mission, Vision & Values, we are ready for the building blocks of our business structure. These strong pillars have to be in place to properly support a Spirit of Enterprise Throughout the Ranks. The first pillar is a principle related to internal employee interaction. It is to Destroy Politics.

In all business settings people have "bad hair" days.

Destroy politics — admittedly, that is strong language. When I say politics I am not talking about prudent diplomacy. I am addressing the interaction among people that causes self-doubt and absorbs emotional energy. Negative politics will erode a **customer success** environment faster than any other single company weakness.

In all business settings people have "bad hair" days. Let's take two peers who are under stress. We will call them Jim and Ann. Jim is in the midst of resolving a difficult customer problem. Ann needs Jim's attention, now, prior to making an important decision. Their high stress moments collide. They have the beginnings of a conflict.

Typically, there is no work rule that requires fellow employees to resolve a conflict. Conventional wisdom says, "Just have a stiff upper lip and move on." Unfortunately, that is not how things play out with Jim and Ann.

The friction intensifies and their business relationship erodes. Jim builds up his "Kingdom," while Ann establishes her "Queendom."

He rallies his allies to form against hers and she establishes a network that opposes him. He defames her and she slanders him. Previously overlooked quirks are highlighted. Two weeks ago these people shared a mutual respect. Now, they are adversaries looking for a way to expose each other's weaknesses.

If they are both candidates for the same promotion, the best person won't win. The least manipulative and least politically adept of the two will lose. Let's say the loser is Jim. If he is influential, he will persuade his comrades of the corporation's unfair and evil ways. Ann moves on, but is always looking over her shoulder.

What happens to the tone of these two employees when a customer calls? The attitudes harbored by these employees will leak to the customer. Ever wonder why a well-organized customer service program is next to impossible to maintain? If you don't destroy politics, politics will destroy the fabric of your organization.

> If you don't destroy politics, politics will destroy the fabric of your organization.

In our company, we nip this type of behavior in the bud. It is a job requirement to resolve an offense as soon as practical. Unless there is an emergency, it must be handled before the close of business on the day of the conflict. This is how we do it.

The two people in conflict must get into a private office and close the door. There is a high possibility the entire matter is based in faulty communication. One party initiates the conversation with four words, "I may be wrong." She then continues, "I was just trying to get a piece of information that only you possess. In my view you were unnecessarily gruff with me. Did I perceive this incorrectly?"

The other person must respond with humility as well. "I may be wrong. I didn't mean to convey any malice. I am so focused on this project that I might have been abrupt, but I sure didn't mean anything by it ..." Usually, it stops right there. In thirty seconds we have intercepted the establishment of two enemy empires within our midst.

🌾

Negative politics
will erode a
customer success
environment faster
than any other
single company
weakness.

I understand you might be skeptical about this tactic. However, since 1991, we have had very few actual closed-door sessions in our company. The strict requirement of the destroy politics principle eliminates most problems at the source.

But what if the discussion above did not result in an amiable resolution? What next? The immediate supervisor functions as the referee. He listens to both sides privately, and then brings them together and resolves the problem. He is skilled in arbitration, due process, and getting to the heart of a matter. He knows how to ask good questions and bring resolution, not simply determine a winner. The victor doesn't get the kids while the loser gets the boat. These rare situations are used to strengthen our corporate culture.

What if there is still no resolution? If one of the employees continues to feel that his complaint was not properly managed, he can elevate the arbitration all the way up to the CEO.

A grievance procedure can be abused by employees. They could use the process to drain their supervisors. The business of business stalls. Leadership can ensure this process destroys politics rather than establishes them. If the process is elevated, the leader's first question is: "What was the result of stage one? How did you start your first sentence?"

There is a simple reason for this. As a **customer success** principle it reduces the chance of your employees interacting with your customers in this way: "How's it going?" asks the customer. "Oh, so, so. Kind of not fun anymore. Just some internal stuff." One comment like this and the customer is wondering, "What's the havoc?" Two comments like this and the customer may wonder if the grass is greener with your competitor.

There should be no gossip, back stabbing, slander or attempts to negatively impact a fellow associate. We have a procedure that enables relationship concerns to be quickly resolved. The procedure is based on principle.

---

5. Communication

"Unless one is a genius, it is best to aim at being intelligible."
— *Anthony Hope 1897*

The second pillar of our principle-based structure is communication. This is a principle because it is so critical, but it is pretty simple. An expanded dictionary describes a total of five components to communication: *sender, receiver, mode, message and impact.* So many ways to mess it up.

As the *sender*, what exactly is it we are attempting to convey? Do we want to gain sympathy, enlist trust, inspire commitment, share gratitude?

Of course there is a *receiver* with whom I am about to communicate. Who is that person? What is he like? How well do I know him? How busy is he? Communicating to a receptionist can be different than to a CEO.

We often don't think much about the appropriate *mode* for sending our message. We usually assume a fax or email is fine. But that is not always true. For example, we should not email our corporate values to a new employee. Jac Fizenz of USC surveyed a major West Coast bank to discover how their employees wished to learn a variety of pertinent information. In almost every situation the overwhelming preference was from the direct supervisor.

What is the right mode in which to send the message?

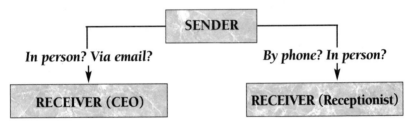

What about the *message* that we are sending? Well worded content is important but I am not talking just about content. What are our reasons for sending the message? To gain support for a critical strategic initiative? To inform people about a new company procedure? To bring correction to an employee in a subtle way? To show that we have taken into account input from an employee? To prove to someone that we are not the ogre that they think we are? Sometimes the subtle reasons and hidden agendas of why we are sending a message can speak louder than the actual content of our message.

Of course we want our communication to have the *impact* that we intend. Did the communication actually motivate the receivers to measurable performance improvements? Are the employees more motivated? Did we really diffuse the conflict that was brewing? Is the quality of service at a higher level? Is there now a more dedicated workforce?

I try not to have any company secrets. I am not suggesting that if you are a publicly traded company, you should share your merger plans. But I am talking about sharing your vision, values, career opportunities, new customers, new services, new marketing plans and operational enhancements. Effective and open communication is a key principle to success.

We want to engage not only the mind but also the heart of each associate. Our employees are our future. If we communicate often and effectively we will build their trust. If we have their trust, we can win their loyalty.

---

6. Focused Alliances

"The secret of success is constancy of purpose."
— *Benjamin Disraeli, 1872*

The Need

Our next principle is focused alliances. This has to do with *concentrating single-mindedly on your corporate purpose*. It is easy to get distracted from your core competencies, since you could probably be successful at anything. But to be exceptional at anything, you must focus.

It was not always this way. At one time, Ford Motor Company owned and managed all aspects of their business directly. It even had its own sheep farm, from which it would take the wool to place in the cushions in the car seats. Over time competition made it unwise to be this fully integrated. Now, they outsource almost everything except car design and marketing.

The seeds of this outsourcing concept were well articulated by Adam Smith in *Wealth of Nations*. In the rudimentary state there is no "division of labor". One man's labor is rarely exchanged for another's.

The individualist must be able to do everything in order to survive. When hungry, he goes outside and hunts. When his clothes wear out, he clothes himself with the skin of an elk or bear. When his cabin begins to rot, he repairs it as well as he can with the trees and turf nearby. (We still have some of these folk making their own way in America!)

> Today, there is a market-driven division more powerful than the division of labor — the division of competencies.

When the division of labor is introduced, the wants and needs of the average person are supplied by the produce of another man's labor. If you prefer to go it alone, you might be able to survive in the wilderness, but not in the jungle of the marketplace. Adam Smith's concept, *the division of labor*, has resulted in productivity gains unimaginable in his day.

Today, there is a market-driven division more powerful than the division of labor — *the division of competencies*. The fastest growing companies are outsourcing everything that they are not experts at performing. Why is this? Agility is the key. Many opportunities make themselves available for what seems like seconds. It is not necessarily the smartest company that wins — just the fastest.

Perhaps this explains a recent Coopers and Lybrand study. They found that companies that outsource non-critical functions enjoy, on average, a 22% faster revenue growth per year than their similar competitors.

Adam Smith initiated the discussion academically. Today, the evidence is overwhelming. You can barely be an expert at one thing, but it is *impossible* to be an expert at everything. The fastest growing, most profitable companies know their bent, and they ruthlessly set aside distractions.

This level of disciplined focus is difficult to sustain. Though we encounter many regulations, some of which contradict each other, technology and success are reducing the power of governments to control their citizens. As a result, business opportunities abound all over the world.

In fact, it could be argued that most enterprises have too many opportunities presented to them. The business leader must discipline himself and his people to maintain focus. He must constantly ask, "Does this new opportunity expand our core competencies? Does this activity sharpen our vision?" If not, he should look for a way to outsource the task to someone else.

To accomplish this, they delegate to others certain functions or operations of the business. *Focused alliances are formal agreements to cooperate for specific business purposes.* This does not constitute a merger. It is merely a well-defined arrangement that enables both entities to better serve a common customer or to expand their customer list.

The Process

There are three practical ways to abide by the principle of focused alliances. First, delegate smartly. Second, avoid distractions. Third, refer business.

On the first component, picture yourself as the champion on top of the hill. In order to stay king of the hill you need some experts in other forms of combat to watch your backside. This occupies enough of your time to fight off the enemies you know. These other experts can fight the enemies outside of your core competencies. If you don't align yourself with experts in other fields, it is impossible to remain king of the hill. To make matters worse, the enemies change their tactics all the time.

To bring the analogy forward, define your backside in terms of cost centers. Cost centers are the areas that must be managed, but regardless of how effectively they are managed, they are not going to generate more revenues for your business. In most companies this includes functions such as payroll, benefits administration, human resource paperwork and software development. Yes, you can do these things in-house, but that requires management expertise, energy, and effort. And it may create undue liability if you fail.

> A focused alliance forces necessary discipline on the company to go deeper with its core competencies, rather than skimming the surface of too many areas.

I am not suggesting that you blindly pay a vendor to manage one of your cost centers. When a function has been delegated you must stay involved. The alliance needs to know how to best serve you. However, I am suggesting that when you have properly defined the areas that do not generate revenues, delegate them.

Second, avoid being distracted. With your focused alliance, look at the customer together, with an eye towards sharing the ensuing rewards. There are companies that have built a heritage in an area that you have not. They enjoy relationship equity with their customers. These are potential alliances. Rather than start from scratch, diversify your service offering and potentially miss the opportunity anyway, link up with an ally.

This does not require trading stock with one another. Simply formalize the way you will serve your common customer in tandem. You get a piece of the pie, the strategic partner gets a piece. This allows each enterprise to focus on what they do best, while both enjoy the benefits of providing a more comprehensive service offering. The result for the customer: great service! The benefits to each business: *a customer who will be more reluctant to cancel the entire package.*

Third, structure relationships which pay referral fees. If a customer calls to ask for a service that you do not provide, but you have a relationship with an alliance that does, refer the business to your alliance. This solves the problem for your customer and you still make something on the deal.

This may sound more like a business strategy than a business principle. Yet it is actually based in a key principle — avoid distractions. This principle helps you to avoid a counter productive diversification that would render an inferior product or service to your customer. This is all about customer success, since the focused company generates more revenue from its niche yielding an ever improving service or product. A focused alliance forces necessary discipline on the company to go deeper with its core competencies, rather than skimming the surface of too many areas.

7. Authority & Risk

"I risked much, but I made much." — P.T. Barnum, 1853

The final business principle deals with the relationship between authority and risk. When we delegate a task to our people, we must give them the authority to carry it out.

Adam (of Adam and Eve fame in the Bible) was given responsibility for naming all of the animals. "And whatever the man called a living creature, that was its name," Genesis 2:19. God didn't come back and say, "Wait a minute, Buster, you can't call that thing a Lion!"

When God gave Adam the responsibility to name the animals, He gave him authority as well. Adam would have flunked the reference check because he had no related experience. God was willing to take a risk.

Whether a business leader heads a department, a small consulting firm, or a multi-billion dollar corporation, releasing control is often difficult. To be successful in the long-term, the business leader must delegate authority along with responsibility.

> If you want your people to provide innovative solutions, they must be set free.

One of the worst dilemmas for any employee is to be saddled with responsibility and not possess sufficient authority to implement the solution. On the other hand, it is quite rewarding to be granted the power needed to manage a project. Granting authority unleashes innovation.

A few years ago, a woman joined our organization as a part-time administrative assistant. She basically filed papers and ran errands. She was loyal, hard working, faithful and conscientious. Over time we gave her increasing levels of responsibility. Recently, we spent a good chunk of change on a fancy piece of equipment and she made the final purchasing decision. Her comment was, "I want to thank you for trusting me with that decision. It is almost overwhelming that you gave me that much authority." What do you think that kind of environment does for employee retention?

By the way, she made a great purchasing decision! She could have made a poor one though. The business leader must embrace risk. Anytime we delegate authority we bear some risk. Even though I prefer not to make any business mistakes, to delegate authority I must embrace risk.

All development, all originality, and all innovation begin with the destruction of something. If you want to build a house, you destroy certain areas of the natural environment. If you want to make one product you consume others. If you want to render a service you displace time or effort. The Austrian economist, Joseph Schumpeter, eloquently demonstrates this reality in his writings.

If you don't have time to read his great works, his theories can be observed in everyday life. Take a magic marker and write something really profound on a white board. Guess what? You have mercilessly reduced the amount of ink that is available to future generations. You may have depleted the magic marker, but you did create something else. This example may be silly, but it is important to understand that risk of loss is necessary for innovation. In fact, with innovation old ideas and technologies become obsolete. Something has to be put at risk to gain the benefit of creativity.

> Something has to be put at risk to gain the benefit of creativity.

So what is my objective with this principle? When business leaders are willing to take risks — as in delegating authority to their employees — innovation flourishes. Often the only direction I give to employees when I delegate is, "What is the best business decision? Go make it happen!"

One of the most important things a leader can do is look in the eye of his subordinate and say, "I trust you. I will support you as long as your actions are in compliance with our philosophy." If you want your people to provide innovative solutions, they must be set free. This does not mean we are lenient on issues of prudence. To the contrary, releasing people puts them on the hook. They are more accountable because they can never use the excuse that they did not have sufficient authority to take advantage of an opportunity.

We will not reprimand an associate for taking a daring position as long as the process was proper. For example, if the employee utilizes our problem-solving schematic he might make a different decision than I would, but it is likely to be a good one. Embracing risk does not imply less due diligence. It does, however, avoid passing the buck.

> This is how talented people in large companies allocate more energy to covering their behind than to generating bold new products and services.

At one of the large companies I used to work for, I was struck by how little power any one person really possessed. A great idea would be conceived, properly documented, and then get referred to another person up the food chain. Though the idea was compelling and within her budget, she would make sure it was supported by someone over her. Amazingly, her superior made sure that enough other fingerprints were on the project that if it ever went awry, it could not be blamed on him. This is how talented people in large companies allocate more energy to covering their behind than to generating bold new products and services.

We all want some level of autonomy. That is why this principle has the side benefit of increasing employee retention. There are few things more rewarding in a work setting than being set free to think outside the nine dots and move ahead with courage to try new ideas. As your employees are free to devise innovative solutions, your customers will be thrilled beyond their expectations.

Fostering the Spirit of Enterprise Throughout the Ranks

"He that will not apply new remedies must expect new evils."
— Francis Bacon, 1577

The mark of a business based on principles is an innovative approach inculcated into the mind and behavior of every employee. John Mill said, "All good things which exist are the fruits of originality." I agree. With the seven principles in place, our people will emanate the Spirit of Enterprise. Our associates will not have to be coaxed into delivering customer service. They will have a passion to make their customers successful.

> Change is not a project in the customer success environment. The spirit of enterprise becomes part of the daily routine.

In our business, the collective energy of our people creates a corporate personality. Our customers talk about our company as if it is a highly respected individual. The energy created by a commitment to these principles is that powerful.

What is the first thing you notice when you come into New York City? The impressive skyscrapers. When you arrive in Prague you are struck with the great spires of magnificent churches. When you fly into Chicago you don't hear a visitor say, "My what impressive foundations this city has constructed." That's because all of us are impressed by what we see first.

The customer is the same way. He doesn't first look at your philosophy statement. He notices the degree to which your receptionist was helpful.

The top of our structure represents what customers observe. How were they treated? Did they feel we owned their concerns? In a business built on principles, the customer might not know what the principles are but he will certainly experience the fruits of their presence. The passion of our employees is the link to **customer success**.

> We are not talking about introducing something new just because it is different. It must trump previous performance.

The key is creating an entrepreneurial mindset. Here is a picture of what is going on in the mind of a **customer success** representative: "Last year, we were able to provide you with a useful service for your employee communications program. And though I am grateful that it was beneficial, wait until I share what we can offer now! I have been thinking about your situation and developed an even better solution. You might have to stretch just a bit to implement it properly, but I think the results will be extraordinary." *Even the customer is being encouraged to think in new ways to improve his situation.* This **customer success** representative has a passion for his customer's success.

Innovative thinking is contagious. We are not talking about introducing something new just because it is different. It must trump previous performance. Often, this is just a tweak of an already well running process.

Initially, I mentioned that this book argues for a way to draw out the innovative element inherent within all of us. Even accountants? Yes, the concept captures a better way of doing things, regardless of the controls and attention to detail required of the job. For example, our CFO outsources certain functions to one bookkeeper in Colorado and outsources others to another bookkeeper in Indiana. He has increased internal controls, decreased costs and streamlined that component of his job. Not bad for a CPA from Kansas, huh?

With the seven business principles firmly established, a passion for **customer success** will be the natural result. There are times an organization needs to be aroused from its slumber and undergo radical change. However, if the status quo is continually challenged, the shifts are caused by all the employees within the enterprise and they appear less radical. Change is not a *project* in the **customer success** environment. The spirit of enterprise becomes part of the daily routine.

The Limits
of Competitive Strategy

W e have been talking about advancing the concerns of your customer through your people. Laying the foundation for **customer success** requires a corporate strategy that is at odds with conventional wisdom.

Michael E. Porter, a highly respected Harvard University business professor, wrote the acclaimed book *Competitive Strategy*. He believes that each organization should fit into one of three boxes. Each box represents a strategy requiring skills, resources and organizational characteristics as summarized below. According to Porter, if a company is not clear about which box it fits in, the company will lose its effectiveness.

Cost leadership requires a large capital investment, process engineering, intense supervision, easy product design and low cost distribution. The low cost producer will also have certain organizational characteristics: heavy emphasis on cost control, very detailed reports, highly structured job responsibilities and incentives based on volume. This company wins in the market place by being less expensive than its competitors for a similar product or service.

Differentiation requires marketing expertise, creative flair, a quality reputation, excellent vendors and service excellence. The organizational characteristics differ from the cost leader rather dramatically. They include coordination of company functions, incentives that are more subjective, employees of a high skill level, amenities and perks for employees and a fluid culture. This company wins in the market place by being better, though likely higher priced, than its competitors.

The *focus* strategy requires skills and resources that are targeted at a specific market. The organizational characteristic is that the entire organization is structured for a niche. Either the cost leadership or differentiation strategy can be enveloped over the focus approach. It wins by attacking a segment, geography or buyer group and penetrates deeply within that niche.

In this analysis, a company needs to engage in a thorough discussion of their strengths, weaknesses, opportunities and threats. This is commonly known as SWOT. They need to ask: What are our strong points? Do we enjoy a strong reputation in distribution, operations, marketing or finance? What are our vulnerabilities? Do we have an inferior product or service? What opportunities lie before us? Can we capture some market share in Houston if we pounce now? What external factor is threatening our livelihood? Is the government about to impose a crippling regulation or tax upon our industry?

The key is that this exercise is conducted *in relationship to the competition.* The company asks: Where are my competitors headed? Where am I now and how can I beat them? And how do I get there? What is their price? What new products have they introduced? Where will they go

> Used as a business strategy, competitive strategy will inherently operate in the past. You are striving to succeed in relationship to what the competition is doing instead of what the customer is saying.

next? What new service delivery mechanism have they structured? The problem is that all of these evaluations are made in reference to the competition — not the customer.

Does the Customer Care About My Competitor?

Competitive strategy is a useful discussion. However, we can not rely on the results to make strategic product and service related decisions. Despite all the hoopla about being competitive, this is a very limited result.

Used as a business strategy, competitive strategy will inherently operate in the past. Here's why: The focus is on your competition. You're always measuring how your competition performed last year or last quarter. Even possessing real time information on your competition will not assist you in **customer success**. You are striving to succeed in relationship to what the competition is doing instead of what the customer is saying.

You can learn helpful things from the competition. The collective wisdom of all the competitors in your industry may help you render a better product at a lower price to the customer. When the competitive environment is free and relatively unhindered, the businesses in that industry get smarter and the customer wins.

For example, according to the Federal Reserve Board of Dallas, to afford a microwave oven in 1947 a factory worker had to work for over 15 months. In 1998, to afford a much better microwave, with more bells and whistles, that same worker would have to work only 15 hours. In real dollars, wages have not increased that significantly. Through competition, the price of a microwave oven has simply come down that dramatically.

Learning from the competition is good. Building business strategy as a result of what the competition is doing could be bad. The reason is simple. You may be running hard to beat your competitor — to the edge of a cliff.

Competitive strategy allocates mental energy and board room resource toward beating the competition. What if you beat the competition and the customer looks at your better product bewildered? He says, "What would I want one of those things for?" Being better than an impressive competitor does not necessarily impress the customer.

Focus vs. Fight

Does the customer cheer you on in your effort to beat the competition? Of course not. The customer couldn't care less. The customer is only thinking about how a service or product impacts her life.

In our industry we offer payroll, human resource services, employee benefits, employer liability protection and government compliance. Some of our larger competitors use a payroll software program that we do not use. Since they are bigger than we are, I could presume that their customers are satisfied with their payroll service. So, I should use the same payroll software package, right? Heavens no. As a matter of fact, according to many of their customers, it stinks.

To ascertain what the customer really needs in a payroll service, I need to ask the customer. By carefully considering the thoughts of the customer, we found they wanted a certain flexibility and format in their payroll processing that the competitors' system does not provide.

The customer provides us with the inputs we need, not the competition. A serious limitation to competitive strategy is that it confines you to *fighting* the competition versus *focusing* on the customer.

Leapfrog the Competition

C ustomer success is not a formula. But the big guys tend to get *formula fixation.*

Try to sell something to a phone company. The line manager may decide to purchase your product. You feel great. Now, this decision will be tested by the legal department, accounts payable, and some purchasing Martian. It can easily absorb a year to get an approved contract prepared for signature after the sales decision has been made. By that time, your company has introduced two newer models, but you fear starting the laborious process again. The line manager you initially worked with has been promoted. The new line manager does not see the need for the outdated product and he squashes the deal.

The best opportunities move at the speed of light. Most big organizations are lucky to move at the speed of molasses.

Compare this process to how the small company does business. The line manager often has the authority to make purchasing decisions with few if any approval signatures. As a result, the sales cycle is completed in less than two weeks.

It is possible to be so big that you block your own view. I am not suggesting that you should throw due diligence out the window in your purchasing decisions. It's just that often the best opportunities move at the speed of light. Most big organizations are lucky to move at the speed of molasses.

> We say, "It is properly structured, therefore it is done." Meanwhile, the fluid, fast-paced company down the street is kicking us in the pants.

The reason that most big companies prefer the security of a set formula is simple: formulas make business processes definable, understandable, and controllable. As business leaders, we like things to be laid out in a nice linear format. That is why we build a customer service department and design a customer service program. We say, "It is properly structured, therefore it is done." Meanwhile, the fluid, fast-paced company down the street is kicking us in the pants.

To fight the disease of formula fixation, we must keep our systems simple, streamlined and flexible. Then we will have the ability to beat the customer to the punch. We should be asking, "What could our customer possibly be wanting from our product or service? How can we deliver an improvement so useful that when she receives it she exclaims, 'Aha! This is exactly what I needed!' "

Merger Mania

As long as two competitors are looking at each other they often wind up asking, "Why not merge?" One company covers the West, the other covers the East and by merging they won't have to beat each other up in the market. Besides, customers are hard to get and even harder to keep.

There are a lot of good reasons to merge. In some settings the customer will actually get a better deal: more services, international scope, ability to migrate from one platform to the next without changing vendors, ability to grow as a business and still have all of their needs addressed. In some environments the demand for rapid growth from investors exceeds the ability of the company to generate the growth internally. The public has given you cash to spend and there are competitors out there just waiting to be scooped up. In some mature industries, the only way to grow is to acquire another company. The market is saturated and everyone else in the industry is forcing consolidation. These companies may have no better alternative than to merge.

> Am I so busy looking at the competition, that I only know what the customer wanted yesterday?

However, it is a challenge to sustain the spirit of enterprise in a merged corporation. The increased policies and structure often squash innovation. New customers were purchased, rather than built. A merger may be necessary, and it might even be smart. Just don't lose sight of your only real corporate asset: the customer!

If I were to merge with some competitor, I would challenge myself with the following questions: Am I so involved in doing deals with competitors, that I have forgotten how to solve problems on behalf of a customer? Am I so busy looking at the competition, that I only know what the customer wanted yesterday?

Innovative Ben

Consider Benjamin Franklin. When he started his publishing business in Philadelphia, he had no money and was relatively unknown. He had just fled his abusive big brother's print shop in Boston. Now he was competing with a wealthy, famous publisher.

When Mr. Franklin began printing his little newspaper, the big competitor decided he would slash his prices and drive Franklin out of business. How could Franklin possibly succeed against such odds? Innovative Benjamin did it by providing information that people wanted to read.

He persistently asked his customers the tough questions. "You have seen my paper, what would you do to make it better?" He'd say, "Here's the leading paper. It only costs you 4 cents. But, what do you find lacking in this publication? Would you pay 5 cents for a paper that had information that you wanted?" He listened and responded to the customers' wishes based on his superior expertise. Of course he became extraordinarily wealthy.

Customer success is a superior corporate strategy. It doesn't fit the customer into a competitive strategy box. It finds out first if the customer even wants a container.

PART TWO

CUSTOMER SUCCESS

Developing a
Customer Success Mindset

O k. You're sold on customer success. You want your customers to call you up and lavish you with praise. You want them to go on and on about how they enjoy being served by your organization. You want to hear them convey how utilizing your services is one of the smartest business decisions they have ever made. You want unsolicited letters of recommendation. You want the next generation of managers at the customer location to use your products or services too.

You are committed. How do you get your employees to follow suit? This next section will present some specific training suggestions. Before providing these templates, allow me to convey my criteria for helping employees to implement any new approach.

- *Begin with the right people or it will fail.* You can be the best trainer and have the best material, but if the employee does not possess basic qualities, it'll go kerplunk.

- *It must be simple to work.* The boss might think it is nifty, but the employee has to be able to understand and realistically follow the steps. More importantly, the direct supervisors must not feel it is too complex.

- *It must have meaning.* If we simply give out new duties we do not change the employee's mindset. Explaining the "why" of the duty is as important as explaining the "how-to".

- *It must be modeled.* The boss has to exemplify the desired behavior. Customer success is more caught than taught. When an employee observes a business leader providing exceptional customer success he will catch the vision.

Hiring the Right People

Earlier, I mentioned that the greatest corporate assets are customers. Many pundits disagree with me. They say your greatest assets are your employees. That sounds nice, but it ain't so.

If an employee leaves your company and the customer remains, you maintain your source of revenue. You can still sell the company since the source of all balance sheet equity is the customer. The customer generates the financial value for the business. The customer is the greatest asset.

That doesn't mean you put your customers first. You move toward customer success by concentrating on your employees. The two passions of a business leader are his customers and his employees. Customers are key, but you must have an obvious desire to see your people succeed to pull off customer success.

Think of your employees as advisors, allies and associates. To possess the best technology in the industry, your associates must support it. To introduce new products and services which differentiate you from your competitor and genuinely satisfy your customer, your allies must rally behind them. To maintain quality assurance systems, your advisors must give you productive counsel. Your employees are the key to implementing excellence.

The Hiring Process

The first step in hiring is so simple we often miss it. *Define the job.* Help a potential employee understand the general responsibilities, knowledge and skills needed. What are the oral and written job requirements? Do they need finance expertise? Do they need to be inductive thinkers?

To complete the job definition, call a meeting with some key employees and managers to ascertain the behavior traits that distinguish the winners from the losers in this particular position. Ask each other the tough questions before you ask the candidate. Notes from this interaction will provide a necessary outline of the position and excellent interview questions.

> The customer is the greatest asset. That doesn't mean you put your customers first.

Now that you know what you need, you are ready for phase two. *Invite as many qualified candidates as possible to apply for the job.* When you advertise, include the components of the job that are behavior related. Advertise your culture. For example, "We're not just offering you a job, we're offering you an opportunity to participate in a creative and innovative work environment." Set yourself apart.

At the time of this writing, unemployment is at an all time low in many cities across the nation. It is difficult to recruit good employees in this environment, but it is possible. Consider developing a Web page. Inquire about possible candidates from businesses which collapse or are downsizing. Pay your sales people a finder's fee when they recruit for you. Provide the delivery man with a job requisition form and ask him to pass it around. Most importantly, become a customer success company and the best candidates will often find you.

As you seek to hire the right employees, have you evaluated yourself?

Do you offer an exceptional array of employee benefits?

Does your pay lead the market? Is it, at least, competitive?

Phase three is the *interview process*. Your well developed questions should weed out those who are not suitable for the position. Make sure that you ask legal questions. A professional employer organization or labor law firm can look over your questions to ensure they will not get you in hot soup. We ask open-ended questions and look for previous behaviors that are predictors of future success.

As the interview begins, build rapport. The first few questions should relax the candidate. This also establishes the interview approach: the interviewer asks questions and the candidate talks — a lot. Listen for values, attitudes, ability to communicate and candor. Does the candidate look you in the eye?

Be wary of the savvy interviewee. Candidates will always attempt to answer questions the way they think you want them to, rather than honestly. Probe. Ask for more detail; listen for more specifics.

As a general rule, only about 20% of the candidates should make it past this third phase.

Phase four narrows it down to **the top two candidates**. This includes another round of interviews with other folks in your organization. In some positions appropriate tests are conducted. If you use tests, make sure you are consistent with the position. Also, have your attorney or professional employer organization ensure that your tests pass validity requirements.

For key people, subject them to a stress interview. This is where the candidate will encounter simulated environments of the worst job-related settings. The candidate may be asked to complete a memo in twenty minutes, while being interrupted by an irate customer. At the same time he is informed of an important sales meeting in fifteen minutes. Watch how the candidate prioritizes under pressure. This provides a reasonably predictable picture of what the person is really like.

In phase five *select the best candidate*. The two candidates that made it past phase four will possess the bona fide occupational qualifications for the job. Discuss the candidates with existing employees who have interacted with them. Select the one who has the superior intangibles: bearing, social mobility, courtesy, depth of character. In politics, many voters apparently think it doesn't matter, but in the real world character counts.

Phase six is the optional *working interview*. You may decide to pay the candidate to come in for a day or two. This working interview allows the candidate to look over your company more thoroughly before providing notice to his current employer. He may use vacation time, but it allows him to assess your culture before making the jump.

On a very limited scale, require real work to be performed. Expose him to many different associates. Ask them to assess whether or not this candidate is genuinely who he seemed to be during the selection process.

Phase seven is the all important *background check*. We want to protect our company against negligent hiring. Does the candidate really have a college degree? Is he a convicted felon?

in a particular job. Past experience may or may not be the best predictor. How he behaved in those previous experiences is an excellent predictor. Here's an example with a sales position.

Behaviors of a Salesperson

Based on our analysis of what it takes to be a successful salesperson in our business, the following behaviors were defined. From these behaviors we were able to develop interview questions which enable us to assess candidates with a high degree of predictability.

Assertive/Initiator: Is the person a doer? Does he attempt to solve problems without lots of prodding? Or is he a procrastinator? I'm looking for aggressive, strong responses that are genuine.

Persuasive/Convincer: Can the person persuade a prospect? Customer? Employee? We'll say, "Here, take this pencil and sell it to me." I'm looking for the establishment of a need, not just the features and benefits. I'm also looking to see if she can close. Can this person change my mind? Can this person develop a need for something I didn't know I needed?

Values/Integrity: Is the person honest and trustworthy? What is his response to white lies? Have his ethics been put to the test in a situation in the past? How does he respond to questions about his integrity?

Empathy/Relationship skills: Does the person get along with others, and can she build long-term relationships? Does she know how to genuinely say, "I know how you feel"?

Ego strength/Conqueror: Does the person have a killer instinct? Is he tenacious? Can he get up when knocked down? Is he absolutely committed to winning? There may be five other sales people in the lobby. Exceptional salespeople love the hunt and the thrill of winning a sale, especially when they do not offer the lowest price. Our service has incredible value, but it is largely intangible. It requires the ability to look the prospect in the eye and challenge him.

Motivated/Driver: Why do you want a career with us in sales? Money should be a part of this answer. A big talker likes to get out and talk to people. Not on my nickel. A good salesperson likes to get out and listen to people and properly determine if a business relationship is feasible — quickly. I'm looking to see if she is willing to subordinate her ability to make a great presentation, for the benefit of closing the deal. Can she ask the difficult questions, even if personally uncomfortable with the question? That shows motivation.

Personal Ambition: If the candidate's motivation is to be a general manager, then I'm not sure I like what I'm hearing for this position. I want a clearly thought out, mature, honest self-assessment. Does this candidate know his strengths and weaknesses? The best candidate knows he can sell and knows he would make a lousy manager.

Customer Success Culture

Congratulations, you have hired an excellent associate! Now you have a golden opportunity to make an excellent first impression. Before you have your new associate fill out a bunch of forms, introduce her to everyone in the office. Assume that she will make significant contributions to the future success of your company, and treat her that way.

When you introduce her make it short, but cover the qualifications. "This is Jane. She brings enviable educational attainments and work experiences. We think she will fit it in well with our culture and provide significant assistance where it is needed. Please make her feel welcome and help her with any questions she might have."

> "We want you to thoroughly understand our culture and our philosophy because we want you to help us preserve it."

After introductions, spend some time explaining what will happen over the balance of the day. "Your main goal today is to get acclimated. We also want you to thoroughly understand our culture and our philosophy because we want you to help us preserve it."

Now take the employee to her desk with the basic employment forms. After she completes the forms, go over the employee handbook and have her sign the acknowledgment form. Explain the health plans, the 401(k) retirement plan and any other pension or profit sharing plans. Give the employee time to digest this information. Attempt to answer all her questions on benefits issues during this first day.

Let the employee spend a little time looking over the shoulder of another associate for an hour or so before you take them out to lunch. Over lunch find out about her family life, her favorite hobbies, etc. Be respectful and laid back. This should not feel like an interview. You should convey genuine interest in your new associate, not just in what she can do for you. After lunch, let her interact with some other employees for an hour or so back at the office.

Sharing Your Business Philosophy

Now it is time for the fun part. Spend whatever time it takes to describe your business philosophy, customer success approach, mission, vision and values. Provide handouts that define these.

> People enjoy working for opinionated people if their opinions are similar.

It is important to be thorough in communicating the most important facets of your company culture. Address questions and provide clarity. Gently instruct your new associate on the salient points of each document. Finally, welcome her support and assistance in maintaining this culture.

We want to retain the people we hire. During the hiring process the candidate should find agreement with our philosophy, but if we made a hiring mistake, or they made a job selection mistake, we want the new employee to find out now. Our business philosophy is rather opinionated and direct. That's OK. People enjoy working for opinionated people if their opinions are similar.

Basic Employee Relations

We want our employees to thoroughly and genuinely enjoy their job and work environment. To do that, they need to treat one another right. The reality is we are attempting to create a culture that is foreign to most businesses and to the communities in which we live. It probably doesn't even exist in many churches and synagogues.

We are cutting against the grain, but the rewards are simply too profound to ignore. As you read this section on basic personal skills it might feel a bit invasive. But let me encourage you. I have been using this approach since 1991 and have received only positive feedback from my employees.

If you have the courage to get a little personal with your employees, the benefit is significant. We do this in company meetings. We are not pointing the finger at anyone in particular. However, all employees understand the environment that is expected. If our attitudes become a bit rusty, we have an entire organization to help hold us accountable. The result is a work environment where not only job performance expectations are clear, but where the rules for relating are clear. This gives our employees emotional as well as financial security from their job.

Lest you laugh, I'm not a "touchy feely" guy. I am a typical, scrappy entrepreneur. Most people prefer an environment they can trust. So do I. We create and maintain an environment that is productive without unnecessary temper tantrums or mood swings. OK, here are the employee relations rules:

- *Expect the best out of your co-workers.* Commit to cooperation.

- *Convey appreciation for your colleague's attributes.* Affirm each other often.

- *Be approachable.* Keep a pleasant expression on your face. It is hard to approach someone who looks grouchy.

- *Listen attentively.* Resist the temptation to plan your next statement while the other person is talking.

- *Wholeheartedly rejoice when a colleague does well.* When you express envy you violate a principle. When someone else has good fortune, go out of your way to congratulate her.

- *Refuse to be moody.* Temperamental people are not consistent. They cannot be relied upon. We all have ups and downs in our personal lives. Don't bring your problems to work.

- *Be humble.* The reality is none of us have all the answers. False modesty is not the solution. It is OK to have a reasonable self-assessment. Just don't be arrogant.

- *Don't gossip.* Critical talk about someone behind their back is destructive. Constructively face the person with whom you have a grievance.

- *Manage stress.* Don't let it manage you. The world is not going to end if you make a mistake. Take a deep breath and face the problem.

- *Acknowledge mistakes.* Correct the error without making excuses.

Customer Success Right Off the Bat

From the first day on the job, there are real life work duties that demand attention. Your new employee is ready to do the job. How can you be sure she will express a passion for customer success right off the bat?

Ingrain customer success quickly through informal role-playing with fellow employees. It doesn't have to be elaborate. One employee acts like the customer, another acts like a customer service representative. In the skit, show that the customer is swamped with work duties. Calling you to get something fixed is just another thing on her to-do list. Though responsive, the customer service representative is clearly not helping her succeed.

At the end of the skit we discuss the interaction. What was wrong with the customer service representative's response? We'll point out that she was courteous, but show how all of her responses were reactive. This leads into a discussion on the superiority of customer success. Everyone pipes in with their thoughts on customer success and the new associate gets a clear picture of how we do business.

After your new associate has started her job, there's still more to learn about your company. Gaining an understanding of your office and company are a part of her ongoing orientation.

This learning process involves a range of fellow associates and the new employee. In fact, since she is a partner-in-training, let her help train herself.

Getting Around the Office

Almost any employee can administer logistics training in less than twenty minutes. It is simple and easy to deliver, yet businesses often overlook it. This can be embarrassing for everyone.

Recently, I called a prestigious law firm that serves our company. They have offices all over the country. I needed their assistance in another state. Not only did the new employee not know whether they had an office in this other location, but she thought they only had one office. I had to persuade her that her firm was national and guide her through the process of helping me.

Do your new employees know where all of your offices are located? Do they know what products and services you sell? Do they know your processes? Do they know your hours of business? Do they know how to use the phone? Train new employees in company logistics early on.

Isn't this obvious? Well, even the most respected companies can oops on this one. I met a gentleman on an airplane who told me a humorous story. He had called Microsoft to get some customer assistance. He must have been connected to a brand spankin' new employee. He asked for some help with Windows. The employee replied with confidence, "Sir, we are not a hardware store, we sell software."

> ✺
>
> He asked for some help with Windows. The employee replied with confidence, "Sir, we are not a hardware store, we sell software."

Your Company Profile

Your new employee needs to learn how you earn a profit. She needs to understand what products and services are the most profitable, and what risks and opportunities you encounter in the marketplace. Many of these details are reserved until your employee has been on line for several months.

Establish the intense value of the customer to your bottom line.

Discuss how costly it is in marketing and service dollars to obtain and maintain a customer. Show that the value of any company is not really its balance sheet assets. It is the source of those assets: your customers. Explain how in many acquisitions the acquiring company purchases the customers, not the stock or the brand name. The customers make or break the company.

Next, convey a profile of the company's customers. Describe how many customers you have, who they are, what they are like, where they are located, what makes them buy from you. Discuss when a customer decides to use your services or purchase your products. For example, is it at a particular time of year, or during a certain time in the customer's life? Remember you are helping your new employee establish a foundation to grip a passion for customer success.

Customer Success Training

As we go through these training tips, reflect on how often company policies or work rules result in poor customer assistance. How often do your customer service representatives say, "We are not allowed to…I'm sorry, sir, that is against company policy…" They may as well say, "I am sorry, sir, my company doesn't trust me to think this one through, so I am going to have to make it hard on you."

Company rules and policies are usually created with good intentions. You need policies for timely payment, contract terms, etc. But do you need as many as you have established? Certain rules can aggravate a good customer, make your employees look foolish and ultimately embarrass the company.

Often a rule is made as a result of being burned in the past. Let's take payment terms. Some customers don't pay you on a timely basis, so you change your payment terms for *all* customers. Now, all those perfectly reliable customers are irritated.

A much better solution is to train your employees to be innovative in their solutions. Teach them how to spot a credit risk. Armed with the right principles and concepts, they can intelligently manage a variety of customer situations.

When we rely on rules, we often make customer-related decisions based on the rules rather than the customer's needs. Think about how this works. Your employees are applying their energy and talent toward obeying the rule, not helping the customer succeed. This is a corporate disease called *rule myopia*.

Customer success representatives are permitted to shift their focus to appropriately solve the customer's problem. In this environment of freedom within the boundaries of proper principles, common sense flourishes.

Give employees guidelines on how to think and behave. You can't establish work rules which cover every scenario anyway. That is why it is important to hire employees who are good problem solvers. Now equip them with the responsibility and authority to handle each situation intelligently.

Consultants not Technicians

It is important for your employees to think of themselves as more than technicians or service representatives. This is not part of an elaborate training program. It is a series of ongoing communications regarding the various components of your service offering. This breadth of understanding enables them to go the extra mile. They are equipped to go beyond the limits of a traditional technician. They function as consultants.

Have three goals for them as consultants:

1. Deliver service so exceptional that the customer is more successful with you than without you.

2. Continually educate the customer on the numerous support services you provide.

3. Cause the customer to understand and genuinely believe that the service fee is inconsequential compared to the added value you provide.

Telephone Savvy

The following are basic rules for relating to customers by telephone. Since so much business is handled over the phone, they are key for customer success. Some companies provide extensive training on how to handle every type of call. That can lead to confusion. We prefer to focus on general principles and basic rules.

- *Answer in person.* The first voice a customer hears should be a live human, not a recorded one. Companies are making a big mistake by relying so heavily on automated voice response. They have no idea how many frustrated customers hang up half way through the maze of automated options. Do not use automated voice response except as a back up when all the lines are busy.

- *Put people first.* Put people before paperwork. Paper can always wait — people should never have to. At the first indication of a customer's presence, put your paperwork down. Make the equivalent of eye contact or focused phone conversation immediately, acknowledging the importance of the customer.

- *Use courtesy and kindness.* Always be cordial. Never say to a customer, "I'm really busy." You are never too busy to give the customer your full attention. Always make the customer feel good that he called you.

- *Employ energetic listening.* Take focused time with your callers. Quick and short answers are intimidating. If the phone rings answer it within two rings, even if you are busy. If you are with another caller graciously ask the first caller if he can be put on hold for just a minute. If the first caller still has a way to go before you can resolve his situation, it is better to call the second caller back than to rush either call. Do not write, type or talk to anyone else unless it pertains to the conversation you are having with the caller. Never eat or chew gum while on the phone.

- *Use clear vocabulary.* Speak on the customer's level. Jargon is confusing to callers and makes them feel inferior. Use plain English. Think about what you are saying before you say it. Articulate clearly and professionally.

- *Practice blind friendliness.* Be friendly even before you know who you are talking to. Answer with a smile. Your tone of voice should always be upbeat. The person on the other end of that line could be the most important customer in the company's history. Convey that kind of attitude.

- *Use common pleasantries.* It used to be everyone said "thank you" and "you're welcome." Now, these common remarks are uncommon. Make yourself stand out. A customer wants to hear that you appreciate his or her business. They want to feel needed. A "thank you" will do that. Saying "you're welcome" will reinforce it.

- *Convey availability to all customers.* "He is in a meeting. Is this a matter you feel is of an urgent enough nature that I should interrupt? Is it acceptable to have him call you back as soon as he is finished? Can someone else be of assistance?" It should not be the customer's job to ask these questions.

- *Avoid backroom descriptions.* Customers are not interested in the mechanics of our business. Provide covered explanations. They are interested in their problem being fixed, not how our copy machine sorts and staples.

- *Always close the loop.* If you are patching a call through to someone else, go the extra mile to make sure the customer is properly connected. If you promise to deliver a message make sure it is delivered.

Empathy

An effective but often missed concept is empathy. Empathy is expressing genuine concern for the plight of another. When we really listen to what the customer is saying, we know what they need and expect. When we don't take the time to listen we are just stabbing in the dark. Here is a simple way to reinforce this concept among your people.

- *How do you know what the customer wants?* Ask her. "What would a satisfactory result look like?"

- *How do you know what the customer means?* Ask her. "You say you want your work environment to be 'nicer'. Could you kindly clarify that for me? What is an example of how it is not that way now?"

- *How do you know when you are helping the customer become more successful?* Know their environment. Visit their location and observe their culture. Expect their point of view to be different than yours. Find out their frame of reference, their context. Ask the customer, "You know what services we render. If you could wave a magic wand, what role would you like for me to play in your business?"

Handling an Irate Customer

R egardless of how exceptional your products or services are, you will still encounter irate customers. We are all human. Even if you are perfect in every way, you have customers who are not. Compounding this reality is the fact that many people think they have a right to be abusive to a company these days.

The general level of courtesy and formality in our culture has declined. Complicating this problem, the common attitude is, "I am the customer and you have a lot of competitors. So, treat me right, because I've got choices."

- *Expect irrational customers.* You may not know if the customer has the potential to be an "A+" customer. (See *100% Customer Retention* for a discussion on grading customers.) So treat all customers with respect and honor. Even if you later decide the company does not want to keep the customer, treat them well now.

- *Respond to their problem as if it were your own.* As mentioned above, empathy understands the customer's problem. That is a good start. The first thing you should say to yourself is, "If I were in your shoes, I would feel the same way."

- *Do not apologize insincerely for something that is not your fault.* That is a customer service technique. Since it isn't genuine, it isn't sustainable. We can still empathize by saying, "If I were in your situation, I would be just as mad, or worse." This often gets the customer to realize they are coming across "mad". In some cases that alone will calm them down. We aren't trying to kill 'em with kindness. We are trying to bring them to life!

- *Ask the customer's permission to solve their real problem.* You should not immediately answer their question. If they are irate, they will not hear what you have to say anyway. Get them to acknowledge that it is acceptable to proceed. The second thing you say is, "May I work with you to resolve this issue?" or "I would like to solve this problem, and I think I can. May I ask you a couple of questions?"

- *Solve the problem.* Follow the process outlined in the problem solving schematic below.

- *Provide closure during the call.* Sometimes you cannot solve the problem immediately. In this case you say, "I will call you back in thirty minutes with the answer. Will that be acceptable?" If you have solved the problem, simply finish with, "Is the solution we just worked through satisfactory?"

- *Close the loop.* Always follow up. If the problem was not solved and you said you would call back in thirty minutes, call back in thirty minutes. If you solved the problem and they said the solution was fine, then give them one last opportunity to prove that they are now OK.

- *Spend the extra minute now to avoid more time later.* "I appreciated the opportunity to work with you on this solution, and I am genuinely glad you called. It is always best to get customer concerns resolved sooner, rather than later. Is there anything else I can help you with?"

Problem Solving Schematic

Y ou can't train your people for every scenario, but you can train them how to analyze. This enables them to solve most any problem. Unfortunately, they probably did not learn how to analyze and solve problems effectively in school. Knowing how to think is a very important component of any job, but it is particularly important when you are dealing with a customer. We try to keep it simple.

We create a thinking environment. Your people are actively involved in problem solving and that sets you apart from most of your competitors. In addition, it broadens the job for your employees. They gain confidence by knowing how to think in a disciplined manner and guide a customer through an intelligent process. This is the schematic we use:

- *Define the problem.* Usually, we attempt to go straight to fixing what we think the problem is based on past experiences. That can be dangerous. Take a few minutes to regroup before defining the problem. Be careful not to allow the stress of the dilemma to outweigh the actual problem at hand. Assess the boundaries of the problem by asking the questions: who, what, when, where, why, how?

- *Test the other side of the issue to help properly define the problem.* Ask questions from the perspective of both parties. Break the problem down into its components. What are the risks? Is there a public relations issue? How would this be viewed by other employees? Vendors?

- *Evaluate alternative solutions.* There is rarely only one way to solve a problem. Look at an issue as if there are at least two solutions. Even if you think the first solution is clearly the best, force yourself to consider an alternative.

- *Critique the alternatives.* Weigh the pros and cons of each alternative. It is very tempting to skip this step after completing step two, but force yourself to be an advocate for the top two alternatives. Think in reverse. You have been biased toward one solution ever since the problem definition phase. Take the other side. Now, seek counsel. No need to reinvent the wheel. At this stage, you should have a clear and articulate understanding of the problem and the possible solutions. Listen to a colleague or superior or subordinate.

- *Select the best alternative.* This solution should feel solid. You should be able to move forward with confidence. There is usually a risk associated with every business decision. That's business. But with this process you will mitigate some of that risk. Now, the decision is yours and you have full authority and responsibility to make the best decision you can. You are smarter than you think. You most likely have made the best choice.

- *Implement the solution.* If it is complex, put it on paper, and then get it done. If it is simple, just get it done.

Confronting Your Enemy

We all have customers that make us uptight. In a brief company meeting, list these customers. Spend five to ten minutes discussing the reasons you do not want to call or visit them. You do not like his disposition. You are afraid to explain the error you made. You think he will be angry. Maybe he always has a complaint, tries to renegotiate the fees or just has an obnoxious personality.

The most important time to talk to a customer is when you do not feel like it. You don't want to return the call. You wonder, "What does he want this time?" Our natural reaction is to delay the bad news. You would much rather avoid the pain of talking to this customer.

Call the customer to address the issues at hand. Call him now, not later. This will actually reduce your stress. You will find out what is wrong and have the opportunity to completely resolve the issue.

Why All The Fuss?

An important criteria of any training program is that it has meaning. As we mature, we appreciate the wisdom of useful rules and adhere to them willingly. Sometimes, companies train employees without explaining the "why". The concept of customer success is so powerful that it usually solicits endorsement on its own merits. We gain an additional edge when we give our employees the following reasons for our approach:

- *It is always less expensive to do the job right the first time.* If you make a mistake, the Company may have to pay a credit or offer a refund. If you make an error, you have to fix the problem and make it right, while concurrently handling other customers' inquiries. This increases the odds of making yet another mistake, starting a vicious cycle.

- *People are screaming for a genuine touch.* The world is more automated than ever. Encounters with people are more important than ever. Humans need a human touch. *Offset our high tech culture with a high touch encounter.*

- *Customers are willing to pay more* for the Company's products and services when they are accompanied by exceptional service.

- *Delighted customers are likely to be repeat buyers*, because they are more concerned about their time than ever. They prefer not to shop around. If properly served, they won't need to. When a customer purchases from you again, without comparison shopping, it dramatically lowers the Company's sales and marketing costs.

- *Thrilled customers will share good news with their friends.* When the customer success approach is taking hold, the customer will trust us with our quality products and services. Their trust translates into a willingness to use their reputation on our behalf. A referral is worth a lot. Think of every service call with that customer's best referral in mind. The customer success in our organization is partly measured by the number of referrals you receive.

- *Customers are not an interruption to your day.* They are the reason you exist. We get so busy working on this project or that report, that we forget the reason we are in business. Customers butter our bread.

Different Strokes for Different Folks

There are a variety of ways to explain these training tips: email, company meetings, skits, one-on-one, one-on-two or three. Use a combination. Resist getting bogged down with one approach. We all have different learning styles. Variety and repetition help your people catch the vision for customer success.

A Manufacturer's Technician

Many people think customer success would not work in a manufacturing environment. The argument is strong: "With so much product out there, we can't possibly be proactive. We have to wait until the customer calls us before we serve him." The following is an example of how I believe you could structure a technician's job in a manufacturing environment.

Don't miss the obvious. Is your product working? If you are a dealer, don't stock products that break down often.

Require service folks to own the product. The best way to ensure that a technician knows how to fix a product is to make him own one. If that is not practical, simulate ownership with periodic scenarios in company meetings at a customer location. Be the customer for a day and see what complaints you would have.

Repair the product before it breaks. Hold technician meetings where they share with each other what is causing the most repairs. Have the technicians problem-solve on the most likely places these repairs could be addressed. Go to those customers and check the potential problem and, if necessary, replace the part.

Allow the customer to determine when they will be serviced. The day of serving customers from 9:00 to 5:00 may still work for the government, but it is long gone from the business world. You may need to hire some folks on a part time basis who are full-time employed at non-competing companies.

Provide incentives for doing it right the first time. In some situations, it is appropriate to impose penalties for not doing it right the first time. Make it obvious that excellent work will be rewarded and shoddy work will not be tolerated.

Beat the Customer to the Punch

You can almost hear the large corporation ask, "Why do these pesky little companies grow so fast?" Their rapid growth defies their distinct limitations. The little company is often undercapitalized, possesses fewer training and development resources, and is limited on executive and managerial talent. Yet, small companies beat the big companies in certain markets every day. In some cases, they set up shop right next door and erode the big guy's market share right out from under his nose.

This phenomenon in American business has repeated itself thousands of times. What is happening? The little guy brings to the market something no one else is thinking about: innovative ways that enable customers to succeed.

They Are Swamped

It's not that hard to beat the customer to the punch because they have so much on their mind. The customer is not thinking about your company for a service-related issue until the problem is severe enough for her to interrupt her day to call you.

Here is what happens. The customer is working on a report and her boss throws four more requirements on her desk and expects them to be completed by tomorrow. Meanwhile, there is this nagging thing going on in the back of her mind. She needs something from you. What was it? She moves on to the next duty and calling your company drifts into her subconscious. Only now she is more frustrated.

She finally finds time to call you. I am not suggesting that you can always be calling your customers in advance of them calling you. I am suggesting that you think about it. If you give *thought* to pre-empting the customer, you will rarely be caught off guard when the customer does call.

They Don't Know

Thinking about the customer — even when the customer is not thinking of you — puts the customer success team in a proactive posture. You are ready for anything.

The customer does not have the level of expertise you have in your product line or area of service. You are the expert and so only you know all the benefits of what you can provide. Here is an example from our PEO business of customer success pre-empting the customer, even when the customer initiated the call.

Let's say Mark calls our payroll department and says, "I would like to change my direct deposit from checking to savings, please." Customer service would politely promise to make the change and say, "Have a nice day. Good bye..." Customer success goes two steps further.

Let's say your customer success representative is Lynsie. She would say, "Well sure, I'd be happy to do that, Mark, but can I ask you a question? I would like to make sure you get the full benefit from what you are trying to accomplish. Could you share with me why you wish to change your direct deposit from checking to savings?"

Mark responds, "Well, I'm really trying to get that 26 week thing through my bank." Lynsie says, "Do you mean the ability to directly deposit your mortgage payment each pay period so you can decrease your principle faster?"

Mark: "Yeah, that's it. My bank makes me put it into this special account and then they take care of it for me."

Lynsie: "Do they charge you?"

Mark: "Yes, but it's only $300 a year and I more than save that back in less interest on my mortgage."

Lynsie: "Do you still need some of your paycheck to go into your checking account?"

Mark: "Of course."

Lynsie: "Is there a convenient way for you to manage those transfers?"

Mark: "Well, it's not bad, as long as I remember to call my bank by phone thing."

Lynsie: "May I share with you an alternative way to accomplish your objectives, without any cost or maintenance on your part?"

Mark: "Sure."

Lynsie: "Well, through us you can have up to 999 different direct deposits off of your paycheck. Since we manage such a large volume, we never charge you for these direct deposits. We can simply send the exact amount you want sent to your mortgage company directly. It does not even have to go through your bank. You can keep the balance of your paycheck going to your current checking account, or any other accounts of your choosing. Would you like for me to set you up with that solution?"

Mark: "Wow, you guys are awesome!" (OK, the customer doesn't say, "You're awesome" every single time.)

Lynsie walks him through the solution and handles as much of the paperwork for him as possible. Then she might take one more minute with him. "Mark, do you have any questions or concerns related to health benefits, your 401(k) retirement plan or how the discount program works?" Often there is one more little thing, but we handle it now, before it becomes a big thing.

How much longer did this take? The customer service person would have hung up about two minutes earlier. Bravo. The customer success person pre-empted what the customer thought he wanted with what the customer really needed.

You Lead the Customer

You will notice that Lynsie led the customer. This is the paradigm shift: *customer success guides the customer.* This might not sound proper, but it genuinely works to the customer's benefit. When you gently lead the customer you provide him with a more thorough and complete solution.

Let's take the example of selling a car. If you are an expert in this field you know more about cars than the prospect ever will. The customer comes on the lot and tells you exactly what he wants. You are doing him a disservice if you sell him that car without challenging him a bit. Perhaps you can properly show him a less expensive, more efficient vehicle that will better satisfy his transportation requirements. Find out what he really needs based on your expertise and guide the customer down that path. Don't just try to sell him the most expensive car, or the car you've been told to push.

Allow me one more example in the professional employer business. When your customer calls and says, "I want to fire Billy," customer service might just say, "OK, we can help you fire Billy". Customer success would drive the solution based on expertise "You know what? We understand your desire to fire Billy on the spot. But we would like to help make sure we do this right. To help mitigate against the possibility of a wrongful discharge lawsuit can I ask you a couple of questions?" We have four pages of them. Those questions help make sure that if the customer is going to fire Billy, the customer is protected.

We don't just want to protect him from being sued. We want to ensure that the remainder of the employees respect him after the firing. By guiding the customer down a path, we serve the customer better and actually help him become more successful.

Sales Staff Helps

Service is not constrained to operations. The folks in operations ensure that the customer is successful, but so do sales professionals. The reason sales and marketing support staff are critical to pre-empting the customer is simple. They will generate ideas that no one in operations would ever see.

We encourage operations people to go out on sales calls when possible, but usually the customer's first interaction with the Company is with an individual in sales. When we sell, we are not satisfied with telling the customer we want their business. We do want their business, but that's not what we want to convey. We want to convey that we want the customer to succeed.

To accomplish this, we train our sales staff to focus on identifying ways to interact with the prospects from a consultant's perspective.

This is how it works. Most sales trainers teach professionals how to handle objections. We train our sales staff to talk to their prospects about risks. There are risks to everything we do in business. What are the risks to employing our service? We help them evaluate those risks as a business strategist. If it is true that there are risks, there must be opportunities. Would you like to allocate more effort to revenue-generating activities?

When the analysis is complete, the prospective customer can decide if the opportunities outweigh the risks. This approach is superior to simply looking at pros and cons. It elevates the conversation to a higher level: making the customer successful. We do not want the salesperson limited to figuring out how to close the prospect. We want the sales cycle to be consistent with the actual service offering. You will find our selling philosophy is simple, straight forward and serves as a useful guide.

Selling Philosophy

The guiding principles by which we will promote our services are simple, but they work and they are supported by the business values.

Knowledge. The customer deserves to know what he is buying. Product and service knowledge is critical in any sales effort, but even more so in industries where a great deal of the selling process is educating the prospect, as in a professional employer organization. Continually acquire knowledge of the service, the laws, benefits, etc.

Be There. Create and maintain a huge pipeline of qualified prospects, and show up. Talk to trusted advisors, employees, owners, etc. in every appropriate market niche. Attend leads groups, appropriate trade associations, etc.

Credibility. Build trust, respect, and rapport with the prospect. Be genuinely interested in the customer's success.

Attentiveness. Empathize, understand their concerns,

Attentiveness. Empathize, understand their concerns, problems, and know their business operation. How do they make a profit? What is an ideal solution?

Discernment. Probe for their real motivations. Ask open-ended questions and listen. Observe what is behind their answer. Enable them to see the need for our service as it relates to increasing profits or decreasing costs.

Integrity. Be truthful all the time, regardless of the short-term cost or potential loss of business — everyone is watching. This is reflected in answering questions directly.

Consult. Discover the customer's business objectives. Understand the prospect's strengths and weaknesses.

Persuade. Explain the risks and sell the opportunities of utilizing our service. Sell to the emotional need, and to their business need, based on their motivations.

Close. Ask for a decision. "Is there anything I have said about our service, which is in any way contradictory to your business practices? Good, may I have your business?"

Personality Profile

Y ou probably never noticed this, but each person is different. There are numerous tools available to assess, define and discuss the way people learn, what values are important to them and why they do what they do. To build a cohesive team, your employees need to have a general understanding of themselves and those they work with. This exercise renders the ancillary benefit of training people to "read" customers. They become more skilled at handling the variety of personalities.

We use a variety of tools, but Carlson Learning Company's DISC test is among the best, in our view. It boasts a huge sample size and provides an accurate assessment of personal characteristics. They utilize an eight-minute test which produces a variety of reports. Essentially, the personality characteristics discussed break down into four basic categories, abbreviated DISC:

1. *Dominance* — this person places an emphasis on shaping the environment by overcoming opposition to accomplish results. This person will cause action, challenge the status quo and solve problems. He might be weak in researching the facts, calculating the risks and understanding the needs of others.

2. *Influence* — this person is interested in influencing or persuading others. She will be a natural at verbalizing, contacting people and generating enthusiasm. She might be a bit weak in speaking directly, focusing on the task at hand and follow through.

3. *Steady* — this person places a high emphasis on cooperating with others to carry out tasks. He will be gifted at developing special-

3. *Steady* — this person places a high emphasis on cooperating with others to carry out tasks. He will be gifted at developing specialized skills, creating a stable, harmonious work environment and performing in a consistent, predictable fashion. He will not be naturally good at reacting quickly to unexpected change, applying pressure on others or conveying flexibility in work procedures.

4. *Conscientious* — this person is interested in working well within existing circumstances to ensure quality and accuracy. She is good at thinking analytically, focusing on details and being diplomatic with people. She needs encouragement to delegate important tasks, to be flexible with policies and to encourage teamwork.

The results of this test become a working document enabling our employees to work together more effectively. And they have more fun doing it. Understanding your own traits and those of your colleagues is helpful in a variety of ways. It helps us not get bent out of shape over little things. It also helps us treat customers with a smile, rather than become angry when someone is different than us. An individual can certainly possess a combination of these characteristics, but usually one will surface as the most prevalent personality trait.

If a high **D** is driving toward the goal, he may be oblivious to a high S's legitimate people-related concern. A high **C** may not feel all the checks and balances are properly in place to accommodate the high I's exuberant plans with a new customer.

This knowledge is useful in customer success training. The **C** is sometimes too rigid. He wants everything to fit neatly in his box. In his view, his box is always superior to his customer's box because he has analyzed all the pros and cons. So, through training, the **C** can become aware of this and be encouraged to embrace alternatives that someone else analyzed.

The **I**, on the other hand, is too fluid. She may not be objective enough in her decision-making. She needs to appreciate details and be trained more thoroughly on closing the loop. The **D** is too fast at making decisions. He can be trained to force himself through the problem solving schematic. The **S** is too comfortable. She may never learn to fly if you don't push her out of the nest. She can be trained to be more proactive at calling the customer.

We administer this test and get together a group of the associates that interact on a regular basis. We discuss each individual in terms of their strengths in front of everyone. We inject humor and generalize when discussing weaknesses. This team training discussion turns out to be great fun for everyone.

There is no superior personality characteristic. We all were born with strengths and weaknesses. We simply discuss these as a group. It enables the team to understand how to work with each other and how to leverage one another's strengths to deliver the best solution for the customer.

Make It Happen!

What makes people successful? Let's look at one of the world's first billionaires, Andrew Carnegie. He obtained his wealth in the steel business, the old fashioned way: by sheer force of will. He only had a formal education through age fourteen. After that, he educated himself vigorously by devouring books on human behavior. He didn't practice everything he preached or learned, but there were a few principles that he followed tenaciously.

He had his weaknesses. He was famously ignorant of steel technology, suggesting his own epitaph should read, "Here lies the man who knew how to gather around him men who were more clever than himself." But he possessed one overpowering strength. He ruthlessly executed his ideas. Execution was the key to his success.

Winning in the market place is not a contest of gathering the most information. It is a battle of will — implementing what we know. We know enough. This section suggested that you train your people to focus on the customer. It is a simple concept, but it has to be implemented to enjoy its benefits.

PART THREE

CUSTOMER SUCCESS

Customer Success
Is Self Sustaining

Wouldn't it be nice if you could establish a mechanism that not only created a customer success environment but also perpetuated itself without artificial props? This is the exciting promise that fostering a customer success mindset can bring to your organization.

This section discusses three components to accomplishing this perpetual motion machine. First, you must provide leadership in how to shrewdly select your customers. Second, a proper incentive system should be connected to any customer success guarantee. Finally, the supervisors at every level must commit to creating a cohesive environment.

100% Customer Retention

How can you really have 100% customer retention? Tough question. Perhaps a better question is, "Why do you want 100% customer retention?"

Grading Your Customers

There are "A", "B", "C" (and worse!) quality customers. An "A" customer pays you a proper fee and genuinely appreciates your product or services. They refer you to everyone they know and you have an excellent rapport with them. "B" customers are almost as good, but may be lacking in one or two of the above characteristics. "C" customers are a different matter.

We don't want every customer we can get. Some customers demand $10 of service for every $7 they are willing to pay. Some customers are just plain ornery. Unfortunately, we have made the mistake of doing business with a rascal or two. In the process of performing a back flip for them, they find something else to bewail. They are so bereft of leadership that they cannot possibly be satisfied. In fact, the customer is abusive. They lie, act rudely and are incorrigible. In some cases, their unethical behavior will put your business in jeopardy. They need a spanking!

It is rare, but if necessary, we will cancel a customer. You might even be tempted to encourage these customers to sign up with your competitor!

Here's why we let them go. The "C" customers will have an adverse impact on your employees' morale. When your employees are overworked and under-appreciated, they may eventually begin to treat even your "A" customers with disdain.

> When your employees are overworked and under-appreciated, they may eventually begin to treat even your "A" customers with disdain.

In addition, the business leader will lose his focus. A few years ago we took on a "C" customer that eroded to an "F-". We were in the infancy stages of establishing one of our offices. This customer became one of the worst distractions in our company's history.

Why did we get snookered into this business relationship? We wanted to establish a presence in this new market so earnestly that it blinded us to the nearly impossible odds stacked against us. Unfortunately, we were willing to look past some of our own business advice to get there. We were set up to fail.

If we had not disassociated with them, we would still be performing exceptional service for this one abusive customer at the expense of the rest of our business. If you end up performing back flips for the "C" customer, two things will happen: you will get no applause and your business will be directed by him, not you.

A large list of "C" customers can absorb so much of your time that they will dictate to you how fast you will grow and how profitable you will become. Most "C" customers eventually go out of business. Where does this leave your business?

That, of course, is the other indicator of a "C" customer. They may have a fabulous attitude and think your services are fabulous, but if they can't pay you, they should not be a customer. This can develop over time. They may start out as an "A" customer and eventually become unable to pay. Identify this early and part ways as friends.

I confess that I learned this lesson the hard way. We serviced a customer who was a pleasure in most ways for four years. Then the customer began to encounter financial difficulty. If I had graciously canceled our business relationship early on, I would have escaped without a scratch. But, I hung in there with him. Though he is a great guy, he simply could not get out of the financial soup. When it was all said and done, he gave me some of his tow trucks. By the time I sold those, I lost money and a significant amount of time and energy.

We do not actually grade each customer. We simply attempt to be watchful in both the sales cycle and in the operations and service setting. We look for certain characteristics that have served us well to date. A new customer must complete an application for services. We may not accept that application. If we bring on a customer and we later learn that we wished we had not done so, we first attempt to fix the customer. That almost always works. In the rare situations when it doesn't work, we terminate the relationship.

Keeping Your Customers

Our definition of 100% customer retention is keeping all of our "A" and "B" customers. If we would ever lose any of these customers to a competitor, we would quickly look at our approaches and service offering. We would sound the alarm and see what systemic problems we may have in our business.

To successfully keep customers, I believe there are five components our employees must live by:

1. *Sell well.* It is important to stick with our core competencies and try not to oversell by setting false expectations. The best way to lose customers is to establish a standard above what you are able to deliver. If one of our salesmen conveys ten things that we can do, but we can really only do nine, what happens? The other nine exceptional services are eventually overshadowed by the one service failure in the mind of the customer.

   Sales is positioning. Proper positioning means skillfully telling the truth. The objective is to persuade someone to buy your product or to use your service based on its actual performance.

2. *Serve well.* Once we have obtained a customer we strive to eclipse their expectations. We do this based on a carefully thought out plan of value-added services we can provide to the customer.

   We go all out to orient the customer to our business. We address any and all concerns and we provide easy access to customer success representatives. The first impression is critical, but we keep it up with surprise extras that make working with us an absolute pleasure. We celebrate our customer.

3. *Coach well.* People are moved to action on the basis of their desire and their belief system. Instill a desire to keep 100% of your "A"

and "B" customers. The worst encounter for a customer is to be confronted with a customer service representative who does not really care if he remains a customer.

Inculcate a belief that 100% customer retention is possible. In sports, what makes the difference in the outcome most often? Talent and coaching. If the talent is basically equal, coaching is what separates the winner from the loser. In particular, the degree to which the players trust the coach's plan determines the outcome.

Kentucky was behind Utah in the 1998 NCAA Final Four basketball championship for almost the entire game. In the second half, they were behind by as much as 12 points, until Kentucky's plan to continually substitute fresh players on the court finally wore down Utah's big boys. Kentucky caught up, but Utah kept it close until the final few minutes. The players believed in Kentucky Coach Tubby Smith's plan. They did not panic and they won.

In the marketplace, we must have a winning plan. The role of leadership is to inspire everyone to desire to keep and to believe you can retain all of your key customers.

4. *Recruit well.* We hire employees who mirror our work ethic and ambition. We enable our employees to think like an owner. This provides them with the responsibility and the authority to perform a back flip for the customer. Even the best coach in any sport must have good talent to succeed.

5. *Retain well.* We motivate our internal staff financially and emotionally, because we believe there is a direct connection between employee retention and customer retention. We do everything we can to keep our people.

Customer retention is not a project. It is a company-wide environment that produces a symbiotic effect: employee retention feeds customer value and customer value nourishes employee retention.

Why is employee retention linked to customer retention? As customers, we are all basically the same. When provided with a choice, we buy from the person we like the best. The same is true with repeat purchases and ongoing service. We like to interact with the person who knows our story and is able to adapt his services to our particular needs. We don't want to explain our needs again and we would rather not have to train another person on how to serve us. When a good employee leaves an organization, two things happen. The customer wonders if there is a management problem "over there", and also loses the person he prefers to deal with.

The vision is to structure an organization which self sustains a customer success environment. To pull this off you need a clear definition of the customer and the service you will render.

The Power of a Customer Success Guarantee

Maintaining any program is difficult. Customer success enjoys a maintenance advantage since it is a mindset, not a program. A *Customer Success Guarantee* can help sustain the excellence in the products or services you sell.

We have devoted extensive effort describing how to uncover what the customer really needs. Now how do we ensure that our associates actually deliver? Lay out the elements of your product or service. Determine which components represent a culmination of your efforts and provide a guarantee on that.

Motivate Employees to Maintain Quality

In our PEO, the guarantee is straightforward enough: We guarantee the accuracy of the payrolls we produce for our customers. If it is not perfect we will grant the customer a credit on their next invoice. The guarantee comes in the form of a personally signed memo with each payroll. This is not a copy. It is a live signature with a real time date. The individual inspector who signs what we call our "Quality Assurance Guarantee" is personally on the hook, since her incentive system is connected to her accuracy. She also has the authority to fix bottlenecks in our organization or system to enable her to achieve the objective.

Anyone can make a mistake. The incentive system is not a penalty. We simply want to highly encourage the associate to ensure that the customer doesn't feel that weakness. If the associate needs to go clear her head a little bit before sending out the payroll package, great. If she needs to take a quick break to get refreshed and then edit the payroll backwards, wonderful. Whatever it takes.

Reduce Business Risk

The customer wants you to be successful, too. It usually takes too much energy for your customer to switch providers. He simply wants a quality product at a reasonable price. The guarantee enables him to see that you mean business about making sure his service is delivered to his satisfaction.

> A guarantee that is meaningful shows the customer your corporate "heart".

Even if you make a mistake — and we all do — the customer will be much more forgiving as a result of the guarantee. A guarantee that is meaningful shows the customer your corporate "heart". You aren't attempting to get something for nothing. You will deliver on what you promised.

The objective of the guarantee is not a marketing tool, though sales folks love it. The benefit of a guarantee is simple: it forces sales and service to collide. The reality is that we are all a bit lazy sometimes. Sales staffers are motivated to get the sale, while service people are motivated to make the operation run smoothly. A guarantee is something that our sales people announce to the world. This builds in a natural form of accountability to the service and operations components.

Be Wise

The guarantee should demonstrate high levels of service commitment. Our guarantees should not impose an undue burden on the employees connected to the guarantee. It must be achievable.

In fact, a guarantee which you cannot deliver on is worse than no guarantee. Let's say you are a phone company. Don't guarantee to a customer that an extra phone line will be put in place in three days if it is impossible to get there in five. The customer may be anticipating the use of a business line in the home. He may even lose a customer by relying upon your faulty guarantee.

This results in an irate customer. It may even establish a liability. If the customer could establish damages, he may be able to sue under detrimental reliance. (That is when someone relies on some performance to their detriment.)

Regardless of whether the customer could sue you for not performing on a guarantee, *be wise* with guarantee selection and implementation. It must be achievable and help maintain the culmination of specified services or product quality. For example, if the phone company established a ten day guarantee and got the job done in seven days, the customer would be delighted.

Solidarity Starts at the Top

To enjoy the rewards of a customer success environment, the management team and all the key business leaders must be in sync. The team that wins is not necessarily the one with the most superstar athletes.

When business leaders work together the rest of the organization can focus on efforts that are in the customer's best interest. This chapter discusses the key ingredients to establish the leadership culture required to achieve a lasting customer success environment.

Have Fun

We really want a great work environment. We don't play pinball during work hours, but we do encourage laughter. There is a difference between fun and play. We do not play at work. But, for crying out loud, the majority of our waking life will be spent at work! So, rather than make work a drudgery, we have to find ways to shape the environment, enabling the grind of the work day to be enjoyable.

Our associates are encouraged to contribute to a pleasant working environment. We do not have a specific incentive system tied to a "fun-o-meter". But since we render a rather serious service, it is all the more important that we find ways to brighten up the work day for each other.

Anyone who has the desire may devise appreciation lunches, birthday celebrations, etc. We encourage this because we want the employees to enjoy one another, but I am not suggesting frivolity. Another word for happiness is satisfaction. To be satisfied with a job well done in an environment where others celebrate your success — that's fun!

Schedule a bit of pleasure mixed in with your business. This starts at the top. Each quarter our key managers and officers get together for a weekend retreat. First we work. We get the majority of our agenda finished before we play.

Then we play. We ski, snowmobile, golf or play basketball. We meet in a nice place, have good food and discuss business issues at each meal. The goal is not to have fun — ski, golf, etc. — but we do have fun. With the proper amount of discipline, the agenda is accomplished. Since we are relating in a different context though, we can really enjoy one another as well as produce.

> ❧
>
> We don't play pinball during work hours, but we do encourage laughter.

When the leaders are together almost anything can be accomplished. The leaders will convey the essence of the enjoyment factor in the way they relate to their subordinates. They do not have to organize a host of fun extra-curricular activities to pull this off.

The leader simply models an excellent work ethic with the right demeanor. He is still serious; he just doesn't take himself too seriously. Like most paradoxical truths, this allows us to be even sharper. Having fun is a responsibility that we take seriously. In fact, it is good for you: "A joyful heart is good medicine." Proverbs 17:22.

It is like the basketball star who goes "unconscious" and doesn't miss a shot. Listen to athletes respond to an interview after an all time high scoring game. They make all of their shots, not because they are super-serious about their technique, but because they are having fun.

Cover Each Others' Weaknesses

We might not want to admit it, but we all have weaknesses. In Part Two, *Beat The Customer to the Punch*, I discuss personality profiles. Since we all know that people were born with different strengths and weaknesses, why don't we accept that fact? Simple. Because one manager thinks he will rise to the top faster if he can exploit the weakness of the other manager. He thinks, "Helping him certainly won't help me."

I realize this goes against the grain of our culture, but we want our managers to be looking out for each other's weaknesses. You probably doubt that this is possible. It is possible — we do it! This concept does not reduce healthy competition in any way. It strengthens your leaders.

I have made it clear that if an aspiring leader wants to enjoy growth, looking out for the other guy is the ticket. As a result, it is in his self-interest to watch the other guy's backside.

To illustrate this point, envision four martial arts gurus defending themselves against twenty big, burly, but untrained bad guys. The four martial arts experts will position themselves strategically. They will have their backs to each other and face the enemy. They know they are on the same team and that their survival depends on each other. By necessity, they communicate extremely well and rely on one another's directives about when to duck and when to hit. They defend the backside of their colleague as if it were their own. If his colleague goes down, his own backside will now be exposed. These trained fighting men will obtain almost certain victory over their opponents if they function as a cohesive unit.

The big, burly, untrained, bad guys represent the obstacles we must hurdle to render the right kind of service to our customers. The last thing our team needs is for one of our "martial arts experts" to bolt on us in our time of need.

We have one key leader who is the most disciplined among us, exemplifying orderliness and follow-through. Another key leader is the most direct, able to cut through issues with clarity and boldness. As these leaders sponsor one another, their corresponding strengths are an inspiration to everyone else. They call each other up and collaborate on customer problems. As a result they are able to reserve all of their energy to repair customer-related issues rather than waste it on dealing with internal antagonisms. Plus, this approach creates an environment where they can work together securely, knowing that the other is not maneuvering for position to their disadvantage.

> The CEO must communicate that one's talent and ability will without political maneuvering, carve out a position that elevates one to his full potential.

This builds a level of trust and service capability that cannot be penetrated. When some outsider wants to point out a weakness about one of your key managers, you can quickly cover for him. This does not mean blithely *covering up* for him, but simply finding constructive ways to compensate for his weaknesses.

The CEO must convey that the ticket to advancement is not beating the other guy. The best way to obtain a promotion is to work hard and focus on making our customers successful. This is particularly true when it involves effectively covering for the weaknesses of your colleague. The CEO must communicate that one's talent and ability will without political maneuvering, carve out a position that elevates one to his full potential.

Loyalty and Trust

What we are really discussing is loyalty and trust. These are long lost principles in the business world. The prevailing *modus operandi is:* "Look out for number one. Your company will not feel obliged to take care of you, so you've got to take care of yourself."

An excellent picture of loyalty and trust is found in the college basketball tradition of North Carolina. Bill Guthridge was an assistant coach for the team for 30 years. The famous head coach, Dean Smith, made sure he retired just before the 1997/98 season got underway. This way he could ensure the administration would have no choice but to allow Bill Guthridge to have a shot at the head coaching job.

Bill Guthridge coached well. In his first year he was named "Coach of the Year" and his team was ranked number one in the country going into the final NCAA tournament. We may have never known what Bill could do had Dean not paved the way for him. True to form, throughout his spectacular first year of coaching, Bill gave credit to Dean Smith.

Almost everyone works below their potential. They may work very hard, long hours, but rarely do people max out on their capabilities. *The business leader's main objective should be to develop his people to a level that they otherwise would not have attained.* When the employees realize that this is the leader's intention, they engage in useful collaboration with their peers.

Unfortunately, it seems most people are afraid of developing their lieutenants. Perhaps they believe they will be out-performed. What could be more rewarding?

Go Team!

Allow me to suggest how powerful a unified team can be in a company. Sports statistics are rampant with modestly talented teams who marshal their efforts toward the goal and beat a team full of superstar athletes. The superstars spend too much of their time competing amongst themselves. While seeking individual glory, they lose the game.

Consider 1,000,000 dry thin sticks. Taken individually, my little girl could break every single one. Put these sticks in one very tight bundle. The strongest man in the world could not break even one. So, who is stronger, my little girl or Arnold Schwartzneggar? Depends on how you pick the fight. If your enemy can divide you then he doesn't have to be that strong to conquer you.

The business leader's passion should be to unleash the collective creative capability. A computer can only do so much. Humans are made in the image of God. They have the capacity to invent based on someone else's preference. So focus on unleashing all of the capabilities of your people. It will thrill your customers!

Please address
your comments or questions to:

The Personnel Department, Inc.
1465 Kelly Johnson Blvd., Ste. 310
Colorado Springs, CO 80920
Toll Free (888)532-1777

The Personnel Department, Inc.
4600 S. Ulster Street, Ste. 700
Denver, CO 80237
Local (303)740-6656

The Personnel Department, Inc.
8275 Allison Pointe Trail, Ste. 370
Indianapolis, IN 46250
Toll Free (800)731-1735